THE LONE ASSASSIN

THE LONE ASSASSIN

The Epic True Story of the Man Who Almost Killed Hitler

Helmut Ortner

Translated by Ross Benjamin

SKYHORSE PUBLISHING

10 9 8 7 6 5 4 3 2 1

Library of Congress Cataloging-in-Publication Data:

Ortner, Helmut, 1950-
    [Einzelgänger. English]
    The lone assassin : the epic true story of the man who almost killed Hitler / Helmut Ortner ; translated by Ross Benjamin.
        p. cm.
    Translation of: Der Einzelgänger.
    ISBN: 978-1-61608-383-0 (hardcover : alk. paper)
    1. Elser, Johann Georg, 1903-1945. 2. Anti-Nazi movement—Germany—Biography. 3. Hitler, Adolf, 1889-1945—Assassination attempt, 1939 (November 8) 4. Germany—History—1933-1945. I. Title.
    DD247.E6O8813 2012
    943.086092—dc23
    [B]

                                2011049214

ISBN: 978-1-61608-383-0

Printed in the United States of America

For Ulla and Jennifer. Who know why.

Contents

Life levels all men. Death reveals the eminent.

— *George Bernard Shaw*

CHAPTER ONE

The Arrest

There was a light fog on the border. The customs officer Xaver Reitlinger gazed over the bushes to the mesh fence, which looked peculiar in the glow of the arc lamp. "If we put the chairs here, we'll be able to keep an eye on the area and hear the speech," said Reitlinger, waving over Zapfer, a young assistant customs employee who had been assigned to him two days earlier. Zapfer moved the two chairs under the window, and without a word, they sat down, leaning their carbines against the house. From here they could survey the whole patrol area: the garden of the Wessenbergian children's home, 250 yards parallel to the border and no wider than 50 yards. Here there was no passage. "Green Border" was what the customs officers called the border strip.

For four years, Reitlinger had done his duty. In that time, he had experienced no serious incidents. But now, ever since the war had begun, deserters had been escaping to Switzerland. Occasionally, he would imagine arresting one of those illegal border crossers. Then he would wonder whether this desire arose from the persistent boredom of patrolling for hours or from his secret need for something unforeseen, something exciting to happen for once. Perhaps it only concealed the deep longing for recognition. A word of praise at some point for one's work—who didn't need that? But how could he be praised if nothing ever happened at the border? Making his rounds along

1

the border fence, Reitlinger would lose himself in his dreams. As he spent hour after hour looking at the same houses, trees, and hills, it seemed as if time stood still. When the mood seized him, he told his wife about his thoughts and dreams. A few weeks earlier, he had told her over breakfast of a dream he'd had that night about the arrest of a man.

"It seems to me that you need a change, or else you'll keep fantasizing," she had said to him, shaking her head.

After breakfast that day—even though it was his day off—he had gone to the customs house to tell the head guard, Trabmann, his dream.

"You should do night watch sometime, more happens on it than during the day, if anything happens," Trabmann advised him. A stout man who didn't look his fifty years, Trabmann recounted how he himself had caught two illegal border crossers several years ago down at Kreuzlinger Tor with a colleague. "They were trying to get over the fence, but we were faster," he said proudly. "But what did we get for it? A warm handshake." Trabmann smiled sardonically.

Yesterday, having long forgotten the matter, Reitlinger had been called to the head guard's office. Trabmann asked him whether he still wanted to do night duty, as a colleague was out on leave. Reitlinger immediately accepted. That day he had reported for morning duty with Zapfer from eight to twelve. After that routine work, he was off until the start of night duty at eight o'clock in the evening. At half past seven, Reitlinger and Zapfer met at the Löwe, next door to the customs house. There was talk of politics and the fact that the Germans needed *Lebensraum* (living space). The owner of the tavern cried, "Certainly, how else should our people sustain itself?" Young Zapfer nodded his assent.

After eating, they went to the customs house and took their carbines from the shelf. Reitlinger was given night binoculars by the head guard, and they set off for their patrol area. "Tonight we won't be bored," Reitlinger told Zapfer, as they walked slowly along the border fence. "I've spoken to the children's home director, and she invited us to listen to the Führer's Bürgerbräu speech."

They sat on chairs in front of the open window and looked across to the border meadow, which was somewhat obscured by wisps of fog in the air. Inside the children's home, under a picture of the Führer hanging on the wall of the bare room, the staff was attentively following Hitler's speech from the so-called *Volksempfänger*, the people's radio receiver. Noticing with surprise that the light was on, Zapfer asked, "Why is the light actually allowed to be on here?" Reitlinger, who was moving his head to the right and left at regular intervals, lowered his binoculars from his eyes. "Tonight they have to turn out their lights on the other side; it alternates every evening because of the enemy. After all, we don't want to make it easy for them here in Konstanz. Those are the orders. Tonight them, tomorrow us." Zapfer was embarrassed to have asked the question; as a soon-to-be customs officer, he should have known about that. But Reitlinger wasn't unforgiving, which set Zapfer's mind at ease.

From the radio boomed Hitler's forceful voice.

> *Our will is just as indomitable in the outward struggle as it was in the internal struggle for power. Back then, I always told you that everything is conceivable, with one exception: our capitulation. And today, as a National Socialist, I can only repeat before the world that everything is conceivable—a German capitulation, never! To those who tell me, "Then the war will last three years," I reply, let it last as long as it will. Germany will never capitulate—not now and not in the future . . .*

"Never!" cried a voice in the room. The listeners pounded on the wooden table with the palms of their hands. The two customs officers were more pensive, neither of them saying a word. The clock on the wall now showed that it was half past eight, and visibility had improved. On the Swiss side, two streetlamps could be seen burning; their beams reached the border fence. When Reitlinger looked to the left for a moment, he thought he vaguely perceived the figure of a man moving toward the Swiss border. Was someone there? He raised his binoculars to his eyes. Indeed, the man had now stopped and was looking around warily.

Reitlinger nudged Zapfer with his arm and handed him the binoculars: "Look, do you see that man?"

Zapfer held them before his eyes: "We have to go there; there's something fishy going on there . . ."

Reitlinger reacted gruffly: "I'm going. You stay here." This was his job; he bore the responsibility. He jumped up and went down from the terrace toward the pear tree near the fence. The man was still standing motionlessly, as if he were listening to noises.

Reitlinger crept up to him from behind. "Hello!" he shouted at him. "Where are you heading?"

The man swung around. He answered with a stammer: "I think I've gotten lost."

Reitlinger looked into his face—a long, soft face, beardless, with almost-shy eyes. He stepped back a few feet and scrutinized the man. He was of small stature, thin, and wore a coat but nothing on his head. His hair was slightly wavy and combed back. No, this man did not seem aggressive . . .

He seemed to recover swiftly from his fright. With a calm voice he emphasized again that he'd lost his way. "I'm looking for a man named Feuchtlhuber, but I don't know anymore exactly where I am."

Reitlinger was confused for a moment. No one could stray here inadvertently; that could only happen intentionally. Who roams around in the dark on the border? "Well, you can't look here, there's no one here," he replied tersely. "Do you have identification papers? Please show me your papers."

The man reacted immediately and reached into his left coat pocket. Reitlinger looked intently at the stranger's hands. Was he about to draw a weapon? Take him by surprise? He held his breath. The man awkwardly pulled out a red border-crossing card. In the glow of his flashlight, Reitlinger saw immediately that the card had long since expired—issued by the passport office of the Konstanz city council for a period of two years, 1933–1935, to the name Georg Elser.

"Is that really you?" Reitlinger asked skeptically. The photo on the card showed a young fellow dressed in traditional costume, holding an accordion in front of him.

"Yes, that's me," the man answered, nodding vigorously.

Reitlinger looked over to Zapfer, who was still sitting in front of the window and waiting for some sign from him. He felt uneasy. On the one hand, this man didn't seem at all dangerous—he actually seemed timid. On the other hand, he couldn't imagine that he was nothing but a harmless border crosser. Hadn't he had that vision in a dream a few weeks ago? Hadn't it been almost identical to the present situation? Hadn't the dream also been about an illegal border crosser? Had it been a prophetic vision?

He turned again to the man: "Can you really play accordion?" he asked with feigned interest.

"Yes, that's my great passion. I enjoy it very much," he answered with a slight smile.

Meanwhile, it had become clear to Reitlinger that he had to bring this man, who claimed to be Georg Elser, to the supervisory office with as little trouble as possible. He patted him reassuringly on the shoulder and said, "This is a completely harmless matter. Come with me now to the supervisory office. An older colleague of mine is on duty there, and he'll definitely be able to give you information about the man you're looking for." The thin man nodded absentmindedly. Reitlinger called over to Zapfer: "I'm going ahead with him to the supervisory office. You stay here; I'll be right back." Zapfer gave a wave of acknowledgment, content to stay, as he would be able to continue listening to the Führer's speech.

Reitlinger told the man claiming to be Georg Elser to walk on his right side—with good reason. The customs house on Kreuzlinger Strasse was about 150 yards away, and scarcely 30 feet away on his left was the border, running parallel to the narrow path. On his right side was a row of gardens enclosed by wooden fences, so there was no escape to the right, and to flee back the way they came was impossible as well. He had deliberately instructed Zapfer to stay at his post, for the man would run directly into his arms if he made a break for it. Nonetheless, Reitlinger was relieved when he arrived at the customs house. Border policeman Mauer, a wiry Gestapo officer who was on duty tonight, was stepping out of the house to get some fresh air.

"You, Mauer, come here!" Reitlinger called to him. "This man here is looking for someone named Feuchtlhuber. He got lost down by the border. Do you know any Feuchtlhuber?"

Irritably, Mauer pointed at the door. "Let's do this inside."

The customs house was a two-story ramshackle building. On the second floor lived customs inspector Straube, whom Reitlinger didn't like, finding him unpleasant and boastful. The house had two entrances: one for Straube's private apartment and another for the customs investigation office. The room was bare except for a table, a telephone, chairs, shelves, and a picture of the Führer on the wall.

Reitlinger showed Mauer the red border-crossing card: "You should search him again. I have to go back up to the patrol area."

Mauer gave him an annoyed look. "Finish your own business! What do I care about this man and his Feuchtlhuber or whatever his name is . . ." Crossly, he gave the man back his border-crossing card.

Reitlinger shrugged. "It's not my affair. I brought the man here; now it's your turn . . ."

"We'll go over to the main customs office. The rooms are brighter there. Here you can't see anything," Mauer grumbled, pointing to the ceiling lamp, which only barely illuminated the room. The three of them left the house. Reitlinger walked ahead, followed by the man, who seemed quite small in comparison to his guards and hadn't said a word in the past few minutes. Mauer walked behind him.

The building that housed the main customs office was the last one on German soil; Switzerland was less than fifteen yards away. There was no barrier. Often the Swiss customs officers stood in front of their customs house and looked across. In the past they'd often talked to each other; on cold winter nights they would offer each other warm tea and cigarettes. They had been colleagues, but in recent years, they'd had scarcely any contact, and since the outbreak of the war, they hadn't exchanged a word. The officers stood silently opposite each other.

Now, too, as Reitlinger and Mauer told the man to enter the customs office, their Swiss colleagues were silently watching them. "Go inside!" commanded Reitlinger. The man stood wordlessly before the steps and looked across to the Swiss side. Did he want to escape? With a few swift bounds, he could do it. Reitlinger simply pushed him through the door. He then asked Mauer to keep an eye on the man for a moment and informed the head guard, who had his office in the next room and was listening to Hitler's speech on the radio.

"Trabmann, I think I've made a good catch. Come over, we have to search someone," Reitlinger said with a hint of pride, bursting into the office. Both had to laugh. They remembered their conversation from a few weeks earlier. The visions in the dream . . .

"Well, then let's go," replied Trabmann, rising from his chair and going ahead to the investigation room.

There the man stood. He looked around timidly as three uniformed men stared at him: Mauer, Trabmann, and Reitlinger.

Trabmann stepped up to him. "Now, to begin with, remove all your clothes and take out whatever is in your pockets."

Hesitantly, the man emptied his pockets and put the objects one by one on the table: a handkerchief, the border-crossing card, a picture postcard of the Munich Bürgerbräu Beer Hall with a Nazi Party stamp, a wallet with five reichsmarks, and all sorts of brass parts—a mainspring, little screws, and a small aluminum tube.

"What's this?" asked Reitlinger, gesturing toward the paraphernalia.

"My God," the man explained haltingly, "I'm a tinkerer. I always make things like that, I collect all sorts of . . ."

Furiously, Trabmann shouted: "You're lucky I don't smack you! Do you think I don't know what those are?"

The man fell silent. Slowly he began to undress. He was wearing a light-colored, slightly worn suit. As he went to hang his jacket on the door hook, Reitlinger noticed a pin under the lapel—a balled fist, the sign of the Red Front Fighters League.

"Why are you wearing that insignia?" asked Trabmann.

"Well, out of foolishness," came the meek answer.

"And why do you have a Bürgerbräu postcard with the party postmark with you?"

"Out of sympathy!"

Shaking their heads, Reitlinger, Trabmann, and Mauer looked at one another. What sort of fellow was this? Gets lost in the dark by the border, is carrying an expired border-crossing card with him, has conspicuous small parts in his pocket that could serve as bomb detonators, pins an illegal communist insignia on his jacket. A madman? A boaster? Or really a harmless man who had only lost his way down here by the border?

Trabmann went over to the telephone and dialed the number of the customs assistant Obertz. "Call the Gestapo. There's a man here for them to pick up; this is their affair . . . and pack up the objects here on the table," he commanded tersely. Then he left the investigation room with Mauer.

* * *

Reitlinger went back into the adjacent room, where he had put down his loden cloak, the carbine, and the binoculars shortly after his arrival. As he prepared for duty again, he looked through the crack of the door into the other room. There stood the man he had caught scarcely an hour ago in the border meadow. There he stood, stripped to his underwear, freezing, timid. He seemed forlorn. For a brief moment, their eyes met.

Reitlinger left the customs house and walked back in the dark to his patrol area, where Zapfer was waiting for him.

Who is this man? The question went through his mind. Who is this Georg Elser?

CHAPTER TWO

The Assassination Attempt

The Badenweiler March resounds in the Munich Bürgerbräu Beer Hall. Cheers burst out. Three thousand uniformed men thunderously shout "Heil." The mood reaches its boiling point. The hall and gallery have been packed for two hours already. The waitresses have trouble bringing the filled beer mugs to the thirsty throats. Now, at eight o'clock in the evening, the noise swells. The Führer has arrived.

* * *

Munich, November 8, 1939: In the "capital of the movement," Hitler meets with his "old fighters," as he has in the previous years to commemorate the sixteen "martyrs" who died on November 9, 1923, for his premature national revolution. Since the National Socialists came to power, this day of remembrance for the "fallen of the movement" has been among the especially important dates of the Nazi holiday calendar.

On November 8 and 9, 1933, ten years after the failed putsch, Hitler celebrated for the first time in the circle of his faithful the memory of the dead of 1923. On that occasion, he began his speech with the statement that he had acted ten years earlier "on behalf of a higher power" to eliminate the "disgrace of November 1918." To liberate November 9 from the odium of a failed revolution and lend it the aura of a "national deed" had since become the leitmotif of all his November speeches in the Bürgerbräu Beer Hall. The propagandistic objectives Hitler revealed in his speech of 1936 were also in keeping with this theme.

> *I want to honor these dead men as the first martyrs of the National Socialist Movement: sixteen men who fell in their faith in something completely new, which first became reality ten years later. Sixteen men who marched under a completely new flag, on which they took an oath, which they sealed with their blood. These sixteen have made the greatest sacrifice. They deserve that the National Socialist Party, and with it Germany as a whole, shall celebrate that sacrifice on this day for all time, over centuries and millennia, and thus always remember these men.*

But what happened back then on November 8 and 9, 1923? What are the events that Germany as a whole should remember? What memories brought together these "old fighters," who now, on the evening of November 8, 1939, wait in their brown shirts, crowded together in the hall, for their Führer to inaugurate the annual celebratory ritual with his speech? And, finally, what did this room—concealed behind the unassuming façade of the Bürgerbräu Beer Hall in the Munich working-class district of Haidhausen—have to do with the events of that time? What made it into a place of worship?

* * *

In January 1923, French and Belgian troops marched into Germany and occupied the Ruhr area, arousing the ire of numerous Germans whose political sentiments had been influenced by the consequences of the Treaty of Versailles. Immense reparation claims by the victorious powers of the First World War had led to inflation and mass unemployment. This had a particularly significant impact on the workers, whose social situation worsened from day to day. Those times of economic, social, and political instability saw the formation of anti-republican groups and associations that were averse to the Weimar Constitution, opposed to the social democrats, and driven by the idea that Germany had to regain its "ability to defend itself," develop an "honorable" foreign policy, and restore its state authority through a strong regime supported by the army.

In Bavaria on September 26, 1923, the government declared a state of emergency and appointed the governor Gustav von Kahr to the rank of general state commissioner. Kahr—who saw himself as a German patriot and whose political ambitions had long extended beyond Bavaria's borders—was only waiting for the escalating chaos to secure the involvement of the army in distant Berlin for his plans. There had been prior contacts and secret meetings with conservative nationalist forces. The three strong men in Bavaria—von Kahr; Reichswehr General von Lossow; and the commander of the Bavarian police force, Hans Ritter von Seisser—were united in their desire to defend "Bavaria's freedom" and liberate the German fatherland from the traitorous republican government.

They were not alone. They had armed organizations at their disposal that, if parts of the Reichswehr would join them, could carry out a successful, organized, and—in their view—long overdue revolution from Bavaria.

The forces around Hitler, Göring, and Röhm—which had gathered in the National Socialist camp as well as in the Kampfbund, a radical right-wing league, and were themselves planning an overthrow—thought the same way as von Kahr and his allies. To seize the upper hand, Hitler and his followers were firmly resolved to beat them to the punch. November 8, 1923, seemed to them a favorable date. On that day, Kahr intended to explain his political goals at a rally of the "national" associations at the Bürgerbräu Beer Hall in Haidhausen. He had chosen the date deliberately, as five years earlier, on November 8, 1918, the German Kaiser had been called upon to abdicate the throne. The following day the Social Democrat Scheidemann proclaimed the republic—from the nationalists' point of view, a moment of the deepest disgrace in German history.

Hitler and his followers had carefully prepared the putsch. Pistols, rifles, and hand grenades had been brought from secret weapons caches in the environs of Munich to arm the participating troops. It was not a small group of right-wing extremists who were

11

determined to carry out the coup, but a large number of divisions, units, and companies that stood ready for the imminent combat operations: 1,500 men of the Munich SA Regiment, whose leader Röhm had previously obtained the necessary weapons via completely official channels under the guise of holding a night exercise with his men; 125 men of Stosstrupp Hitler—Hitler's own assault squad—who were also members of the SA; 300 men of South Bavarian SA units; and 2,000 fighters of the Bund Oberland, formerly the Freikorps Oberland. Two infantry units were provided by the paramilitary group Reichskriegsflagge; another 200 loyalists of the Munich Kampfbund stood ready to mobilize, as well.

To avoid the impression that General State Commissioner von Kahr was afraid of Munich citizens, the organizers had taken only the most necessary security measures for the Bürgerbräu Beer Hall event. The two nearby police stations were each reinforced by 13 men to guard the gathering. In a barracks only five hundred yards from the Bürgerbräu, another 45 police officers stood ready. Thirty officers of the Munich central police station were deployed to ensure order and calm outside the venue. About 150 men were posted inside the hall to watch over the event, supported by 12 police detectives who took up positions in the hall and on the gallery. Many of the police officers sent as security were themselves National Socialists.

As Kahr was just beginning his speech, in which he would present a fiery critique of the 1918 November Revolution, Hitler and his faithful were approaching the beer hall in a red Mercedes. Shortly before eight o'clock in the evening, they arrived, and Hitler gave the on-duty police officers the order to clear the area in front of the beer hall of visitors who had not been admitted. Though Hitler possessed no authority at all, the officers began to drive back the crowd into the connecting side streets. Then the units of Stosstrupp Hitler arrived in several trucks. They surrounded and sealed off the Bürgerbräu. Now it was time for Hitler's grand entrance. With a loaded revolver in his hand and surrounded by a group of armed comrades, among them Rudolf Hess and Hermann Göring, he entered the packed hall. There was a sudden commotion as numerous visitors attempted to leave the hall quickly through side doors. Their efforts were in vain, for the putschists had blocked all doorways, positioning machine guns in front of them.

To quiet the room, Hitler, wearing a black frock coat, shot his revolver at the ceiling. He then stormed through the rows of tables to the speaker's podium, pushed von Kahr aside, and shouted: *The national revolution has just broken out! The hall is occupied by 600 heavily armed men. No one is permitted to leave the hall! The barracks of the Reichswehr and police are occupied. Reichswehr and police are already approaching under swastika flags.*

This was not, in fact, the case. Neither were the barracks of the Reichwehr and police occupied, nor were soldiers and police officers approaching the Bürgerbräu Beer Hall under swastika flags. It was Hitler's first speech in the Bürgerbräu that evening, and after he had given it, he told Lossow, Kahr, and Seisser to follow him into a side room. Since Hitler was armed and apparently prepared to shoot, they listened to him grudgingly for about fifteen minutes.

As an ultimatum, Hitler declared: *Everyone has to occupy the place allotted to him. If he does not do so, then he has no right to exist. You have to fight with me, triumph with me, or die with me. If things go wrong, I have four shots in the pistol: three for my colleagues if they abandon me, and the last bullet for me!* Next to Hitler stood his burly bodyguard Ulrich Graf, a butcher by trade, with a submachine gun at the ready. Outside the window of the side room patrolled SA units.

Meanwhile, out in the hall it had grown quieter. Göring had calmed the crowd: *Relax, relax, you have your beer!* he shouted repeatedly. Excited and intimidated at the same time, the visitors waited to see what would happen next. Suddenly Hitler reappeared on the podium, having left the side room due to the faltering negotiations with Kahr, Lossow, and Seisser. *If there is not quiet right now, I will have a machine gun posted on the gallery!* he screamed into the hall. He then began another speech, seeking to win over the unsympathetic crowd. An eyewitness later described those minutes.

He began with complete calm and without any pathos. What was happening, he said, was in no way directed against Kahr, who had his full trust and would remain in control of Bavaria. At the same time, however,

13

a new government must be formed: Ludendorff, Lossow, Seisser, and he.
I cannot remember ever in my life having experienced such a reversal in
the mass mood in a few minutes, almost seconds . . .

Hitler declared that the government had been dissolved. The same day, a new Reich regime would be proclaimed in Munich, and until the reckoning with the criminals who led Germany into dissolution, he would assume the leadership of the provisional government, in which Ludendorff would be head of the Reichswehr, Lossow would be Reichswehr minister, and Seisser would be Reich police minister. It was the task of the provisional government to muster all the forces of Bavaria and the rest of the Reich, march into the "sinful Babel" of Berlin, and save the German people. Hitler admitted that it had not been easy for him to induce Kahr, Lossow, and Seisser to join the new regime, but they had ultimately consented, and he asked the people in the hall whether they approved of this solution to the German question. The crowd roared its assent.

General Ludendorff applauded, too. He, who had come to the beer hall late to avoid unpleasant encounters and now appeared in full uniform and bedecked with medals, certainly did not have in mind playing a subordinate role alongside Hitler, a mere lance corporal. Nonetheless, he declared that he was at the disposal of the national government. He wanted to restore to the black, white, and red cockade the honor that the revolution had taken from it. This was, he stated, a turning point in German history, and he trusted in God's blessing for the undertaking. After that, Kahr, who had in the meantime been permitted to return to the hall along with Lossow and Seisser, stood up and went to the lectern. At that moment of extreme need, he said, he was prepared to take over the management of the affairs of the Bavarian state as representative of the monarchy that had been so disgracefully shattered five years earlier. He did so with a heavy heart and, *I hope, for the benefit of our Bavarian homeland and our dear German fatherland.*

Enthusiasm seized the crowd, which erupted in cheers and applause, and then everyone joined in the concluding German national anthem.

In the belief that the revolution had succeeded, the following proclamation was promptly published.

To the German people! The government of the November criminals in Berlin has today been declared deposed. A provisional German national government has been formed. This consists of General Ludendorff, Adolf Hitler, General von Lossow, Colonel von Seisser.

Triumphantly, Hitler then left the hall with his people. From that point on, General Ludendorff took over the command on-site, and—to the later chagrin of the Nazi putschists—he released the three coerced men on their word of honor.

As soon as Kahr managed to free himself, he hastened—along with the head of the Bavarian Reichswehr, Lossow—to the barracks of Infantry Regiment 19, where they renounced the forced participation in the Hitler putsch that same night. The Munich Reichswehr garrison was mobilized against the revolutionaries, and the National Socialist Party was banned. The next morning would bring the ultimate decision: Kahr or Hitler?

That night, Kahr had posters printed and posted all over Munich, on which he accused Hitler of breaking his word and declared the liquidation of the National Socialists, as well as the Bund Oberland and the Reichskriegsflagge.

The morning of November 9, 1923, SA columns and members of the Kampfbund, including the Bund Oberland, gathered at the Bürgerbräu Beer Hall, far superior in numbers to the police. Opposed to them stood the police units of the city, the state, and, if necessary, the Reichswehr. The putschists had not expected to meet such massive resistance. The more clearly their defeat loomed, the more desperate their actions became. Thus, "Marxists" from the Munich city council were taken hostage at Göring's orders, without knowing what would happen to them. As "strategic measures," cannons were positioned at various points in the city center. At the same time, the attempt was made to bring the city's most important military and political institutions under control. Except in the case of the Wehrkreiskommando, the military district command, the putschists failed miserably. Neither the police headquarters nor the government offices on Maximilianstrasse could be occupied.

The destruction of the social democratic newspaper *Münchener Post* exemplified the National Socialists' lack of a cohesive plan. At Göring's explicit command, the publishing premises were occupied, the editorial offices were ravaged, and machines and material were destroyed. When everything lay in ruins, Hitler's "order" came to preserve the editorial offices. He had planned to transfer the printing and publishing apparatus to the National Socialist newspaper *Heimatland*, but it was too late.

The situation for the putschists was increasingly hopeless. Something had to happen, and once again the attempt was made to turn things around. To achieve the national revolution, they decided to march through the city center; the destination was the Feldherrnhalle (Field Marshals' Hall). The putschists assembled in three columns and four rows. In its entirety, the procession, twelve men wide, filled the whole street—to the left the Stosstrupp Hitler, in the middle the Munich SA Regiment, and to the right the Bund Oberland. At the head marched the Führer and Ludendorff, in front of them a guard division and two rows of flag bearers.

Initially, the Nazis managed to break through the first chain of state police at the Ludwigsbrücke. However, at the Feldherrnhalle, a barrage from the police ended the overhasty "march on the Feldherrnhalle." An eyewitness recalled the event.

A rattle of dozens of shots rings out, penetrating the ranks, shattering the procession. An indescribable panic ensues in the densely packed masses, which now burst apart, as if a gigantic hand had broken in and dispersed them. Women start screaming, men are shouting, dozens have flung themselves to the ground to evade the bullets tearing into the crowd. Dozens, hundreds push their way out of the range of the devastating fire.

Sixteen National Socialists would ultimately pay for their march with their lives. The putschists' Führer got off lightly himself: Hitler dislocated his shoulder when he either fell down or was thrust down to the pavement. Göring was wounded, brought to a Munich hospital, and afterward smuggled across the border by party members.

The putsch had failed. What had been publicized as the ignition point of the national revolt had evaporated into a brief delusion. But the fire still sprayed dangerous sparks. When police units drove up in front of the Bürgerbräu Beer Hall on the evening of November 9 to free the imprisoned hostages, they were berated by the furious public: "Traitors to the fatherland! Bloodhounds! Heil Hitler!"

Two days later, the police appeared on Lake Staffel at the country home of Hitler's close associate Ernst Hanfstaengl to arrest the escaped Führer. Shortly before the arrival of the police, Hitler reached for his pistol and cried: *This is the end. I will never let those swine arrest me! I would rather die!* Hanfstaengl's wife then knocked the weapon out of his hand; Hitler's end had been prevented, but the sparks he struck had not been extinguished.

* * *

On November 8 and 9, 1933, the National Socialists, who had then come to power, commemorated for the first time their fallen "martyrs" of 1923. They met at the historic place where they had once proclaimed the "national revolution," which now, ten years later, had become a reality—the Munich Bürgerbräu Beer Hall. The ceremonies began on November 8 with propaganda events in the Munich city center, culminated in a two-hour speech from Hitler to the "old fighters" in the Bürgerbräu Beer Hall, and were crowned with a memorial march to the Feldherrnhalle and the swearing-in of SS recruits. An eyewitness from 1933 described the "historic march" from the Bürgerbräu in Haidhausen over the Ludwigsbrücke to the Feldherrnhalle.

It was doubtless an impressive demonstration: the serious men in brown shirts, the silent crowd, and the burning pylons on the façades, all against the background of the gloomy November weather. As the procession reached Marienplatz, the chimes of the city hall played the Horst Wessel Song. Gun salutes announced the arrival of the head at the Feldherrnhalle. A minute of silence followed.

That evening, a bronze memorial was solemnly unveiled at the arched side opening of the Feldherrnhalle. Hitler demanded of the recruits that they, too, sacrifice their lives for the "national revolution," *just like the sixteen who fell here at this site. For you there must be nothing in life but loyalty. . . . These dead men are your model . . .*

From that first commemoration onward, the rituals were established. The National Socialist leaders and their "old fighters of 1923," who met annually in the Bürgerbräu Beer Hall, staged a celebratory event, which primarily served the recasting of the 1923 fiasco as a patriotic act. The outcome of their trial after the putsch attempt helped them with this falsification of history. Most of them got off scot-free as mere hangers-on who were "just following orders," while the ringleaders received mild sentences. It was helpful that the judges quite openly sympathized with the putschists. Hitler was sentenced to a five-year imprisonment in a fortress, counting the pretrial custody. After just under a year, he was free. His struggle could begin anew. The fire could be reignited.

*   *   *

Hitler had not forgotten his comrades-in-arms from those days, especially not those who had given their lives. They were depicted as "blood witnesses to the movement" and declared "martyrs." The "Blood Order" decoration remained reserved for the participants from that time. In 1934, the Führer buttoned it to the right breast of their uniforms. From that moment on, they wore it with pride— as they do now, at the Bürgerbräu event on November 8, 1939.

The blood-red ribbon, attached to the button of the right breast pocket, stands out conspicuously from the brown shirts. On it hangs a solid silver medal, which shows the profile of an eagle perched on a wreath and bears the inscription: *9 November, München, 1923-1933.* On the opposite side of the medal is an engraving of the Feldherrnhalle. Above it is a swastika surrounded by sunrays, and written in an arch the words: *Und ihr habt doch gesiegt* ("And you were victorious after all").

"Yes, we were victorious. We were there when the national uprising began in this hall. We fulfilled our patriotic duty." That is how they think, the men who wear their medals proudly on their breast. As in all the previous years, it is their celebration, their evening.

As the Führer, followed by prominent National Socialist figures, strides to the podium, where the microphones are set up in front of a large swastika flag, enthusiastic cheers burst out. "Heil, Heil!" The shouts resound through the hall. Reflected in the faces are excitement, pride, and even awe. They are all assembled before Hitler: in the front row the prominent party figures, behind them the "old fighters" and the surviving comrades of the sixteen "fallen of November 9," national and regional party leaders, SA and SS officers, labor leaders, and other party members. The hall is bursting at the seams.

The Führer speaks, and the Volk listens. The party members here in the hall are not the only ones listening; throughout the whole Reich, people sit at their radios and follow the speech. It is noteworthy that Hitler, on this evening, limits the usual "story of the party" to a few passages and that his speech instead amounts to little more than a single incendiary tirade against England. To frenetic applause he blames England for the outbreak of war.

The forces that stood against us in 1914 have now once again instigated war against Germany, with the same platitudes and with the same lies . . .

If Lord Halifax declared yesterday in his speech that he champions the arts and culture . . . then we can only say: Germany already had a culture when the Halifaxes still had no inkling of it. And in the past six years, more has been done for culture in Germany than in the past one hundred years in England . . .

For I have sought to develop not only the cultural side of our life, but also the domain of power, and have done so thoroughly. We have built up our armed forces—I can safely say so today—so that there are none better in the world . . .

England as a creator of culture is another story. We Germans certainly do not need the English to show us anything in the realm of culture.

Our music, our poetry, our architecture, our paintings, our sculptures can absolutely compare with the English arts. I believe that a single German—let's say, Beethoven—achieved more musically than all Englishmen of the past and present together!

19

The hall roars.

What they hate is the Germany that is a dangerous example for them, the social Germany, the Germany of our social labor legislation. The Germany of welfare, of social equality, of the elimination of class differences—that is what they hate! They hate the Germany of social legislation, which celebrates the first of May as the day of honest work!

And, of course, they hate the strong Germany, the Germany that marches and takes upon itself voluntary sacrifices.

His tirades are repeatedly interrupted by enthusiastic applause. With a forceful, piercing voice, he goes on.

Our will is just as indomitable in the outward struggle as it was in the internal struggle for power. Back then, I always told you that everything is conceivable, with one exception: our capitulation. And today, as a National Socialist, I can only repeat before the world that everything is conceivable—a German capitulation, never!

To those who tell me, "Then the war will last three years," I reply, let it last as long as it will. Germany will never capitulate—not now and not in the future . . .

They will by no means be able to defeat us either militarily or economically. There can be only one victor, and it is we!

The applause following the speech lasts for minutes. It is as if the crowd is intoxicated. What they are celebrating with shouts of "Heil" is the belief in their own invincibility.

Even as the national anthem resounds, bodyguards clear a way to the exit for Hitler and his entourage. In their jubilant revelry, most people in the hall at first don't even notice that the Führer has already left the place of worship.

* * *

Due to "urgent affairs of state," Hitler had initially wanted to forego his annual speech in the Bürgerbräu Beer Hall. He had decided only the day before to participate in the traditional event after all. His debate with his generals on the matter of the western campaign formed the background for his hesitation.

On October 22, Hitler had decided to launch the attack in the west and scheduled the beginning of the offensive for November 12. The generals of the army were of the opinion that an attack before the spring of 1940 would not be feasible, and they opposed Hitler's plan, but all their attempts to dissuade him from it failed. Due to the unfavorable weather conditions, the date then had to be postponed nonetheless, and the attack preparations already set in motion had to be stopped. Now Hitler intended to make a final decision on the new date on November 9, and he wanted to stay in Berlin in order to keep holding the reins in this matter.

Thus the celebration had originally been planned with a scaled-down program. Hitler himself did not want to give a speech. Instead, his deputy Rudolf Hess was to speak on all German radio stations on November 8 at 7:30 in the evening. But then everything was changed. In one of Hitler's typical spontaneous decisions, he flew from Berlin to Munich to give his speech, despite the time pressure. The organizers were instructed to shorten the evening program so that Hitler could take the night train to Berlin that same evening. He wanted to be back in the Reich Chancellery the next day. Since his private pilot had not been able to guarantee him a return flight to Berlin that evening in light of the uncertain weather conditions, a special train had been provided for the return journey and its departure time had been scheduled for 9:31 PM.

Most people in the hall know nothing about all this. They only noticed with surprise that the Führer had spoken more briefly than in all the previous years and afterward immediately disappeared. Most of them now make their way to the exits. Only the "old fighters" stay and drink beer together. The clock shows that it is 9:20 PM.

While Hitler is on the way to the train station with his entourage, a bomb explodes in the Bürgerbräu Beer Hall with a deafening blast. Beams crack, masonry breaks, dust clouds up; screams and panic ensue as part of the ceiling caves in. Seven people are immediately dead. Another will die on the way to the hospital. Over sixty people are seriously injured. The Bürgerbräu Beer Hall now resembles a heap of rubble.

Meanwhile, Hitler, who was the target of the attack, is boarding the train to Berlin. In Nuremberg, he receives the news of the bomb attack. His first reaction: *It's a false report.* Later, he declares: *Now I am completely calm. The fact that I left the Bürgerbräu earlier than usual is a confirmation for me that providence wants to let me reach my goal.*

On the evening of November 8, 1939, the myth of providence guiding and protecting Hitler is born. The editors of the National Socialist newspaper, the *Völkischer Beobachter*, write their propaganda articles that night. The next morning, they appear throughout the entire country under the headline, "The Miraculous Salvation of the Führer."

The assassination attempt, which from the evidence suggests foreign instigation, immediately provoked a fanatical outrage in Munich. For the identification of the perpetrator, a reward of 500,000 marks has been offered, which has been raised to 600,000 marks by a voluntary private contribution. The devastating explosion in the Bürgerbräu Beer Hall occurred around 9:20 PM, at a time when the Führer had already left the hall. Almost all the leading men of the movement at a national and regional level had accompanied him to the train station, where he boarded the return train to Berlin immediately after the conclusion of his speech due to urgent affairs of state. It can only be called a miracle that the Führer escaped with his life from this assassination attempt, which is at the same time an attack on the security of the Reich.

But who were the assassins? Who were the "nefarious murderers"?

CHAPTER THREE

The Interrogations

The call came shortly after nine in the evening. Police assistant Otto Graeter was just about to turn off his radio. The Führer's speech, which he had followed with his colleagues Roderer and Jankow, had been surprisingly short. Jankow, who was on telegraph and telephone duty that night, picked up the receiver. "Graeter," he cried, "someone has been arrested at customs. We have to head over!"

Graeter looked at Roderer grumpily. "Let's go," he said, and they went outside and got into a gray Volkswagen. The drive from the former Villa Rocca—a well-maintained, three-story house from the late nineteenth century in which the Konstanz Border Commissariat was housed, located in the middle of the city—to the customs office on Kreuzlinger Strasse took about twenty minutes. Graeter, who was forty-three years old and robust in stature, had been transferred at the beginning of the war from the criminal police to the border police. Here he served in Section II, Internal Political Affairs—a subdivision of the Karlsruhe State Police Department. Customs dealt with imports and exports and guarded the border. But if anything out of the ordinary occurred, then that was his business.

"What's going on?" Graeter asked, after he had entered the customs house with Roderer.

Mauer, a young Gestapo officer who had been detailed to customs as reinforcement, approached Graeter. "We have an illegal

23

border crosser," he said tersely, pointing to the adjacent room. There sat a small, inconspicuous man, with a gaunt face and a timid look, dressed only in a shirt and pants. He was wearing a simple shirt without a tie. Graeter approached him. The man was a craftsman; he saw that at first glance. His hands were work-worn and battered.

On the table lay all sorts of small parts: screws, springs, and wires, which most likely came from a clock; a border-crossing card; a wallet with five marks; a sheaf of notepaper; a pocket-knife; a pair of pincers; and a small piece of hard-cured sausage. There was also a postcard showing the Munich Bürgerbräu Beer Hall on the table. Graeter could not make sense of this. He instructed Roderer to pack the paraphernalia in a small box. Only after the customs assistant Obertz—who had come over from his room—had drawn attention to an insignia that the man wore on his lapel did Graeter's face light up. "Ah, a Red Front Fighter; look here . . ."

Then he cast a glance at the border-crossing card. It had expired. He looked at the photo, read the name. "Your name is Elser?" he asked sternly.

"Yes, Georg Elser . . ." the man answered in a calm voice.

"Then let's go!" Graeter shouted with a wave of his hand. He said good-bye to Obertz and Mauer and left the customs house with his driver Roderer. They took Elser between them.

It was about ten o'clock when they returned to the Villa Rocca. Elser had remained silent during the whole drive. A few times he had cleared his throat, and once he had wiped his nose with a handkerchief. Graeter went with him into his office on the second floor, pushed a chair over to him, stuck a piece of paper with carbon copy sheets in his typewriter, and looked across the desk. "All right, friend," he said gruffly, "here we go. Just don't tell any stories, or else there will be trouble."

"What were you doing on the border?" he began his interrogation.

"I didn't want to cross the border. I wanted to visit Herr Feuchtlhuber. He is the chairman of the traditional costume society. On the way I got lost . . ." Elser replied in Swabian dialect.

Graeter became angry: "Don't talk nonsense! No one believes you!" He reached for the telephone to ask a colleague to check whether there was a Herr Feuchtlhuber in Konstanz and whether he was the chairman of a traditional costume society. Minutes later the telephone rang: Yes, there was a man with this name and he was in fact the chairman of a traditional costume society. Only he lived near the Petershausen train station, far from the spot where Elser was found.

Graeter confronted Elser with this fact. He only shrugged. "I don't know my way around Konstanz."

An impenetrable, slippery fellow, thought Graeter—and one who was not to be trusted. He had to know his way around Konstanz, for he had lived there for almost seven years, as a quick check in the register of residents had revealed. But he admitted nothing. For nearly half an hour now, Graeter had been sitting opposite him, asking question after question, but so far he had received only sparse details.

Name: Georg Elser
Hometown: Königsbronn near Heidenheim in the Swabian Alps
Occupation: cabinetmaker
Marital status: single

In addition to these facts, Elser divulged some information about his recent workplaces. Where had he come from? From Munich, no, from Ulm . . . Graeter's patience was wearing thin. He stood up, walked around the desk and planted himself in front of Elser: "Tell the truth! What were you doing on the border? Why did you want to enter Switzerland illegally?" he shouted with a threatening voice.

"I have an illegitimate child and could no longer pay the alimony," Elser answered, intimidated.

Graeter had no doubt that this answer was a lie, too, though he could not verify it at that time. He wasn't sure what to do next. He could not get much out of this man—a stubborn fellow. He knew that the questioning had now reached an impasse.

* * *

It was about eleven o'clock when the teletypewriter began to tick in the ground floor office. *Bomb Attack in Munich*, read the heading. Under it followed fifteen lines ordering an intensification of border surveillance. Jankow brought the message up to Graeter.

"Well, how about that," Graeter said indignantly after reading it, "how about that."

Elser looked at the stunned faces of the two Gestapo officers. He ran his fingers through his hair and appeared quite calm.

No sooner had Jankow returned to his office than a second communication had come: *Attack on the Führer*, read the heading this time, followed by a message stating that all border stations were to be put on alert and suspects were to be apprehended. Jankow was overcome by a strange feeling—might the detainee on the second floor have had something to do with this? After all, they had found a postcard of the Munich Bürgerbräu Beer Hall on him, along with odd small parts that could come from an alarm clock. Didn't you need an alarm clock to detonate a bomb? He didn't want to accuse this inconspicuous fellow of anything. But the fact was that he had been caught in the attempt to cross the border illegally. And finally, he was a communist. Wasn't he wearing that forbidden sign with a balled fist?

Jankow hastened upstairs and showed Graeter the new communication. Without any visible reaction, Graeter skimmed the message, thanked Jankow tersely, and set the paper aside with apparent thoughtlessness. He then walked over to the window; outside the fog had thickened, and the visibility was less than fifty yards. Lousy weather, thought Graeter, fitting for this evening. The police assistant was in a bad mood. Sitting in front of his desk was a man who looked as if butter wouldn't melt in his mouth, and yet his investigative instinct told him that something wasn't right about the fellow. That message . . . he couldn't have had something to do with . . . ?

Graeter suddenly turned around. "An attempt has been made on the Führer's life," he shouted sharply. At the same time, he looked into Elser's face, but the man showed no reaction whatsoever. Seemingly composed, he received the news.

Graeter left the room. From the telephone in the opposite office, he called his boss, Inspector Hinze. "We have here an illegal border crosser who has come from Munich," he reported excitedly. "Yes, he mentioned that he came on the ship from Friedrichshafen." He was instructed to interrogate the man further and inform the state police station in Karlsruhe immediately.

A few minutes later, Graeter called the Gestapo in Karlsruhe and described the arrest of a man named Georg Elser. His orders were to "keep at it, continue the interrogation, pursue every suspicion, and report back immediately with any results."

Graeter went back into his office, where Elser was still sitting calmly in his chair. The man must have nerves of steel, Graeter thought. He opened a drawer to take out a slice of bread for himself. He offered Elser a piece. "Want some? You must be hungry, too. I don't know how much more time we will have to spend with each other today."

Elser shook his head. Only after Graeter offered him a cup of tea from his thermos did he accept with thanks. He didn't become any more talkative afterward, though, and time crawled.

Graeter felt the pressure on him. His boss and the Gestapo wanted results; they wanted to know what was with this Georg Elser. What had he been doing in Munich? Why did he want to go to Switzerland? What was the significance of the things found in his pockets? Did he belong to a group of communist conspirators who had carried out the attack on the Führer and then dispersed and gone into hiding? Graeter had his suspicions, but he lacked evidence and had so far failed to extract a confession.

Meanwhile, the clock showed that it was three o'clock in the morning. Graeter was tired and running out of patience with Elser. He had finally sharpened his tone, shouted and threatened, but all to no avail. Now it seemed sensible to him to lock the man in a cell for the time being. Maybe that would make him more talkative. He brought Elser into one of the three detention cells on the ground floor. Just as he was about the close the iron door, Elser stepped up to him. "Officer, may I tell you something?"

Graeter pushed him angrily back into the cell. "No, you may not tell me anything at all. I don't want to hear anything more from you. I've had enough!" He slammed the door and went up to his office. His anger was written on his face.

That stubborn fellow is not going to walk all over me; tomorrow is another day—then we'll see, thought Graeter. His pent-up anger dictated the content of his report, which he now, as the clock approached 3:30 AM, typed on his typewriter. Half an hour later, he was done with it. His last sentence read: "It cannot be ruled out that Elser could come into consideration as the perpetrator."

* * *

At seven o'clock in the morning, Inspector Hinze appeared in Graeter's office. He carefully read the report, which took up less than one typewriter page. "A tough fellow, eh?" he remarked, shaking his head. He then instructed him to send the report by teletypewriter to the Gestapo in Karlsruhe.

The morning in the Villa Rocca would turn out to be hectic. When the report reached the Gestapo in Karlsruhe, it was immediately forwarded from there to Berlin. Due to the communication from Konstanz, the Gestapo launched a blitz operation that same night. Registers of residents were investigated, Elser's background was determined, and, to the extent possible, his life up to that point was reconstructed. There was nothing suspicious to be found, but the Gestapo did not give up. Even as Graeter was talking to his boss in Konstanz about what to do next, the Gestapo had criminal police in Königsbronn, a small village in the eastern Swabian Alps, arrest Georg Elser's parents and siblings and bring them to Heidenheim for questioning— once again, to no avail. "Georg is supposed to have been involved in the attack? No, he was never particularly interested in politics . . . he's a hardworking, quiet person. Most recently he worked in Munich . . ." There was nothing more to be learned from the interrogations.

The scarce information gathered by the Gestapo officers was immediately forwarded to Berlin, where the secret state police had already received more than 120 leads on suspicious people after the first night. They sorted through them and sent them on to Munich for further investigation. There, in the "capital of the movement," an army of criminal investigators under the leadership of Kriminalrat and SS-Oberführer Nebe had begun their work, overseen by Himmler himself.

The officers pursued hundreds of clues. They sifted through the ruins of the Bürgerbräu Beer Hall, searching relentlessly for parts of the explosive device that might produce a lead on its origins. The staff of the Bürgerbräu Beer Hall was questioned as well. Maria Strebel, who had worked as a waitress on the evening of November 8 and had suffered hearing damage from the detonation of the bomb, later described the circumstances of the interrogation.

The next day—I was lying at home on my sofa at 23 Pariser Strasse on the second floor—a police detective came. He asked me to come with him, but I refused, because my daughter was still very little. She was nine years old at the time. In the next room, my mother lay dying. A few days after this event, on November 19, she died. The detective told me that a colleague of his would come soon and ask me to come with him. On November 10, I had to go to the state police headquarters on Brienner Strasse for questioning with my beer maid, a nineteen-year-old Viennese girl. We entered the room.

I saw about eight to ten police detectives sitting at desks, interrogating civilians who had been summoned. As I approached one of the desks, the interrogating officer asked me for my husband's telephone number. He wanted to call him and inform him that I would not be coming home. I told him that that was unacceptable, because I had to return home to my seriously ill mother and my child. Then I went to a certain man on the third floor. This man gave me an official document so that I could pass through the entrance again in order to go home and speak to third parties. In the days that followed, police detectives came with typewriters. They were at my home about five or six times. Again and again they asked me whether anything struck me as unusual. Then, a day or so later, I had to go into the city again to the police station. There I was again questioned. Suddenly the interrogating officer opened his drawer, pulled out a picture, and put it on the table. He asked me, "Have you seen this man before?" I said, "No." But here I have to add that I had seen this man before. He was a guest. He sat in the Bräustüberl [a smaller restaurant attached to the beer hall] every day. The identity of this man came back to me only later, after I had spoken to my other colleagues. I remember that he was very poorly dressed and ordered the normal worker's meal, which had cost sixty reichspfennigs at the time. He caught my attention—and this is the reason I remember him well—because he never ordered anything to drink.

Maria Strebel was not the only one who was visited by the Gestapo the day after the assassination attempt. Waiters and waitresses, barmen, cigarette women, workmen, janitors, cleaning women, and toilet attendants were all interrogated, though without success. Himmler was gradually losing patience; it was high time a perpetrator was found.

* * *

In the early afternoon of November 9, Inspector Hinze's telephone rang in Konstanz. "Bring this Elser to Munich," was the terse order. Hinze called Graeter to his office and asked him to take Elser to Munich. He declined: "I'm simply too tired after the long hours last night. Someone else should take this on."

An hour later, criminal police secretary Wilhelm Moller was driving a gray Volkswagen toward Munich, with Georg Elser sitting in the backseat.

CHAPTER FOUR

One People, One Reich, One Führer

It is so hard to describe all this, sighs the newspaper *Münchner Neueste Nachrichten* on November 9, 1939. *The heart is not resilient enough to grasp the most horrible crime of all time.* Nonetheless, an eyewitness was found who had not lost his pithiness.

> *There is a dull, heavy blast . . . an aircraft bomb? Someone screams the words that are as unforgettable as those moments: "There was an infernal machine in the hall!" That is like a crushing blow and an immediate jolt. The Führer was speaking in there just a short while ago. He spoke much more briefly than usual. . . . An attempt was made on the Führer's life— my God, what bestial brain spawned and committed this dreadful act?*

The witness described to the readers of the *Münchner Neueste Nachrichten* his profound distress.

> *A comrade emerges from the ruins. His face is streaming with blood, encrusted with dirt, and his brown shirt is streaked darkly with blood. He grabs us by the shoulders and cries, "They wanted to take our Führer from us!" He screams this incessantly in anguish.*

The report concludes: *More firmly, more resolutely, and more faithfully than ever before, the whole Volk has now rallied around the Führer.*

One people, one Reich, one Führer—united in the search for the "nefarious assassins." A report from the German News Agency two days after the attack described the status of the investigations into the assassination attempt in the Bürgerbräu Beer Hall.

The responsible authorities have taken all measures to step up the investigation and illumination of the nefarious attack in the Bürgerbräu Beer Hall. In the interest of a central management of this operation, SS-Reichsführer Himmler has assigned the whole task of solving the crime to a special commission of experts. This special commission is evaluating all clues with even the slightest possible connection to their investigations and has already made important findings.

The rescue work for the severely and mildly injured in the Bürgerbräu Beer Hall was carried out as quickly as possible thanks to the exemplary cooperation of all the local forces and the assistance of still-present "old fighters." This deserves even greater emphasis in light of the fact that this rescue work had to be undertaken in the midst of a wild chaos of rubble, ruins, and debris. Among the police, firefighters, Wehrmacht pioneers, members of party organizations, ambulances, etc., there was outstanding cooperation from the first minute of the operation on, so that the great difficulties of the rescue and recovery effort could be managed smoothly.

According to the findings so far, the act was by no means a spontaneously perpetrated attack, but rather a very carefully prepared crime committed with a mechanical timed detonator.

What happened here was not something primitive and born of the moment, which was hatched only a brief time before the rally. Rather, both the choice of the place and the "expert work" suggest that the perpetrators made very careful preparations.

Even if specific perpetrators or groups of perpetrators cannot yet be identified, evidence and leads nonetheless indicate the direction in which further investigative activity should move. Within the scope of this systematic, painstaking work, the collapsed masonry is also being meticulously examined. Only by piecing together the countless individual results of the investigative work can the police reconstruct the bigger picture.

Fortunately, the public in the capital of the movement is taking an immense interest in the illumination of the attack. From all social strata, people are continuously coming forward to provide information and contribute to the solution of the crime by reporting clues.

Under the headline "Valuable Leads from the Public," the German News Agency disseminated another article on November 10.

As the German News Agency has learned, the special commission for the investigation of the crime of November 8 has been receiving more and more clues and statements from comrades belonging to all social groups. For that reason, the special commission has been tripled in size this Friday so that it can process exhaustively the influx of information. Though this contains at present mostly clues of a general nature, it can certainly yield important results. Currently, probably over a thousand such leads have been reported by the public. Just as praiseworthy as the cooperation of all German comrades in the solving of the disgraceful crime is the joint effort of all the members of the special commission from the first to the last man—for they not only feel a strong sense of duty, but are also putting their hearts and souls into it. Currently, experts are in the midst of meticulously investigating the found parts of the mechanical apparatus used for the detonation of the explosive charge. It is essential to this task to determine the exact composition of the metal parts. At this point, it can already safely be said that, with respect to the alloy of individual metal parts, a foreign origin will indeed be demonstrable. There are presently investigations in progress from various sides working completely independently of one another to reach an absolutely sound result. This particular type of investigation is of decisive significance, all the more so as the special commission is already pursuing clues in a quite specific direction, and it can be expected that further details might be made available to the public in the immediate future so that the special commission, which investigates all leads, will receive more information pointing in this direction.

Meanwhile, Georg Elser had already been questioned by the SS officer Nebe in the Wittelsbach Palace. Despite threats and intimidation, Nebe did not obtain a confession.

Gestapo officers of the special commission had their doubts anyhow. For them, a lone assassin was out of the question; behind the deed, they assumed, was a plot—a conspiracy. They were convinced that they had to search for foreign instigators, and they were not alone in this view. The official coverage of the Munich attack aimed from the beginning in the same direction.

On November 9—when the official investigative commission had just taken up its work—foreign instigators were already suspected. The *Völkischer Beobachter* of November 9 stated: *Today we do not yet know in detail how this criminal act was prepared or how it was possible. But we know one thing: the instigators, the financial backers, those who are capable of such a vile, abhorrent idea—they are the same people who have always used murder for political purposes: the agents of the secret service! But England shall get to know us!*

The Bürgerbräu attack, which in contrast to all previous twenty-nine assassination attempts on Hitler had almost succeeded, provoked wild speculations. Was it Jewish circles, communist resistance fighters, or did the evidence point outside the country, as the Propaganda Ministry would have people believe? Was it a joint operation among agents of the British secret service and Otto Strasser—who, as an opponent of Hitler, had founded in 1930 the Kampfgemeinschaft Revolutionärer Nationalsozialisten, an organization of "revolutionary National Socialists," also known as the "Black Front," and had been living since 1933 in Swiss exile? The Propaganda Ministry strove zealously to spread this version.

The idea that it could have been the act of a single individual was beyond imagination. Neither the Gestapo nor oppositional circles believed that. The former would have had no political interest in it; a lone perpetrator, and a German to boot, was of little use for the propagandistic purposes of the National Socialists. And the latter accused the Gestapo of staging the attack itself in order to spread as propaganda the myth that providence had saved the Führer. Both theories of behind-the-scenes manipulators would be long-lasting . . .

*　*　*

In the secret briefings of the SD (Sicherheitsdienst, or security service), the "string pullers" behind the attack were also suspected of being in England. There was method in this. A confidential memo from Berlin urged the Nazi-coordinated press not to direct speculations on who was to blame for the assassination attempt in the Bürgerbräu Beer Hall at domestic German groups. At that time, anything could be of use, with the exception of German resistance groups or an assassin from among the people.

In foreign policy that year, Hitler pursued his goal of the "conquest of German lebensraum," which he had already begun to realize. Austria had been "annexed" to the German Reich since the Anschluss in March 1938. Czechoslovakia had to "relinquish" the Sudetenland to the German Reich; Great Britain, France, and Italy had given Hitler their political blessing for the appropriation of this territory in the Munich Agreement of September 1938. In violation of this agreement, but without protest from the three powers, Hitler had then given the order in October 1938 to seize what remained of Czechoslovakia (the so-called *Erledigung der Rest-Tschechei*). As of March 1939, there was only a "Reich Protectorate of Bohemia and Moravia."

Hitler strove for total domination of Europe. He sought and found the opportunity for this in Poland, where his stated aim was "the expansion of lebensraum in the east and the securing of sustenance." Thus, he asserted, there was "no longer any question of sparing Poland, and we are left with the decision to attack Poland at the first suitable opportunity. . . . Right or wrong or treaties play no role in the matter."

The German-Soviet Non-Aggression Pact of August 1939 with the secret protocol for the division of Poland cleared the way for Hitler's invasion, which began on September 1, 1939, after a staged attack by the SS on the Gleiwitz radio station. Two days later, Great Britain and France declared war on Germany. The Second World War had begun.

From that point on, Hitler's focus was on the western offensive. The date of the attack, originally planned for November 9, had still not been decided, because the generals of the Wehrmacht regarded an offensive as premature in terms of military preparedness.

For the Nazi regime, a favorable opportunity thus presented itself in the wake of the assassination attempt to foment the necessary bellicose mood in the German public with the help of propaganda. As propagandistic raw material, the German News

Agency assembled a collection of purported quotes from foreign media that were sent to editorial departments as proof of foreign "warmongering."

To the editors: The following material, which proves the guilt of the warmongers in London and Paris in the Munich attack, is being made available to the newspapers not for use in the form provided by us but as a basis for commentary.

CHAMBERLAIN declared in his first speech before the House of Commons soon after the British declaration of war: "I have only one wish, and that is to see Adolf Hitler destroyed."

TIMES: "Now it is a matter not of Hitler's conditions, but of Hitler himself."

EXCELSIOR wrote: "England and France have reached the mutual decision to put an end to the bloodthirsty despot Adolf Hitler."

TIMES: "As long as Hitler and Hitlerism have not been wiped out, England will make no peace."

The Member of Parliament SINCLAIRE in the House of Commons: "As long as Germany is ruled by Adolf Hitler, our only choice is either to submit to his will or to eliminate him."

The correspondent of the NEW YORK JOURNAL AMERICAN reported from London: "England has only one war objective: to do away with National Socialism, from Hitler down to the last party member."

TIMES: "In the effort to annihilate the Nazis, some moral values will naturally get lost. Nonetheless, millions are praying that Nazism will be destroyed."

Vladimir D'Ormesson in FIGARO: "France and England must reduce Germany to rubble. We must obliterate the Hitlerite instigators of European wars."

PETIT PARISIEN: "Hitler is faced with a decision: either to depart of his own free will or to be plunged into the abyss."

CHAMBERLAIN: "Peace is not possible as long as Hitlerism continues to exist. We must put an end to it."

DAILY MAIL, twenty-four hours before the attack: "The discussion of war objectives is simply senseless. All that remains for us to do now is to eliminate Hitler."

And as if to resolve any remaining doubts about the participation of British agents, this compilation was followed by the note:

The whole world noticed that the British newspapers were able to report strangely quickly on the attack in Munich. Thus the DAILY EXPRESS could already give a detailed report on the night of November 9, while foreign newspapers that have correspondents in Germany did not yet have any news.

There was no doubt that these propaganda messages would be taken up in media reports and commentaries, for a critical, oppositional press had not existed for a long time. The Nazi policy known as Gleichschaltung—enforced coordination and uniformity, achieved in part through the suppression of politically dissident organizations, especially among the working class and the Jewish minority—had silenced the opposition, driving them into prisons and concentration camps, into emigration or underground activity.

But the Munich attack did not lend itself only to warmongering. As the Nazi propagandists recognized immediately, the myth of providence—the myth of the inviolability and invincibility of the Führer—could also be nourished. The fact that they achieved both goals is illustrated by secret briefings from that time. On November 10, the SD officers on Wilhelmstrasse in Berlin noted:

In many schools, the chorale "Now thank we all our God" was sung. Various factory leaders informed their followers of the attack at roll calls. The public was especially unsettled in the course of yesterday morning, before the particulars of the attack became known. Rumors cropped up everywhere—such as reports that the Führer had been seriously injured and that various leaders of the party and of the state had been killed. As the details of the assassination attempt became known in the course of the day, all the resulting problems were widely discussed. The British and Jews, who are widely regarded as being behind the attack, were discussed with acrimony. In some places, there were demonstrations against Jews. Generally, it is hoped that from now on the Führer will no longer expose himself to such dangers, as he has done often recently.

Furthermore, people are now expecting various retaliatory measures against all enemies of the state and a sudden outward attack on Great Britain.

The German Intelligence Service reported that same day on public loyalty demonstrations in the Reich:

Kassel, November 10—After the nefarious crime in Munich, which has provoked extreme outrage and profound horror in all strata of the German public, over 100,000 comrades gathered in the afternoon hours on Thursday on Friedrichsplatz in Kassel to express their gratitude for the kind providence that saved our Führer and to offer Adolf Hitler a spontaneous loyalty oath of their steadfast allegiance.

On November 13, 1939, another secret report on the internal political situation read:

The Munich attack has bolstered the sense of solidarity in the German people.

The interest of the public in the results of the special commission assigned to investigate the attack is enormous. The question of how this attack could happen is still the main topic of conversation in all circles. The love for the Führer has grown even stronger, and the attitude toward the war has become even more positive in many circles as a result of the attack.

There is a pronounced mood of hate toward Great Britain. The fact that the Führer was present during the funeral services in Munich impressed the general public deeply. The participation of Munich residents in the state funeral for the victims of the attack was relatively low. Only on Odeonsplatz did a crowd of onlookers form, though without showing an especially deep interest in the solemn act.

It was not only the rather passive attitude of the Munich public that was regarded with suspicion. The reactions of the churches were criticized, as well:

It is uniformly reported from the whole territory of the Reich that there have been strikingly distinct reactions to the Munich attack on the part of the Catholic Church on the one hand, and the Protestant Church on the other. In all parts of the Reich, the Catholic clergy avoids taking any position on the event, disregards it as if it had not occurred.

Approvingly, however, the report notes:

In contrast, the Protestant Church has sharply condemned the Munich attack and taken a clear position. In some parts of the Reich, services of thanksgiving for the Führer's survival were held, and in others there were pulpit declarations, which, to single out an example from Stuttgart, had roughly the following wording:

"Distress over the diabolical attempted attack on the life of our Führer still trembles in all of us who have come together today, but the gratitude for God's saving mercy is also great and powerful in us.

"In the rain of bullets of the world war, during the courageous march on November 9, 1923, in the ensuing years of struggle for political power, and now during the diabolical attack, the almighty God has always held His protective hand over him, and we will pray to God each morning to preserve our Führer, give him—and us with him—victory, so that we come to a good peace and our people are granted space to live [lebensraum] *and the possibility to live."*

One people, one Reich, one Führer—perfectly in tune with the Nazi propagandists. Up to that point, the attack had lent itself ideally to their objectives. But what about that illegal border crosser who had been brought to Munich and was sitting in a Gestapo cell awaiting his next interrogation?

In his interrogations with SS officer Nebe, Elser had so far denied the act and generally said as little as possible. Meanwhile, the evidence against him had been steadily accumulating. Employees of the Bürgerbräu Beer Hall who had been questioned remembered him. A businessman who was tracked down—the supplier of the insulation material that was buried in the rubble—also remembered the small man with the Swabian accent. In the meantime, the crime scene commission had pinpointed the origin of the explosion in a column close to the floor of the gallery. The perpetrator must have worked on his knees and presumably did so for nights on end. On his own? Hard to believe. Nebe was certain that there were co-conspirators. But Elser wasn't saying anything.

He didn't name names or provide any information at all. Yes, he had occasionally sat in the Bürgerbräu Beer Hall, he had answered when Nebe confronted him with the statements of the staff, but that was permitted—it was a public establishment, after all.

Himmler was losing patience. If Nebe couldn't manage it, someone else would have to conduct the interrogations. On November 13, Kriminalrat and SS-Obersturmbannführer Huber took over as head of the commission. They had a conspiracy theory. Now all they needed was a perpetrator.

CHAPTER FIVE

The Confession

There was a knock at the door. As two Gestapo officers led Elser inside, he struck Kriminalrat Huber as small and slight. Huber scrutinized Elser, whose alert, lively eyes lent his face a cunning quality.

No, thought Huber, it's impossible—this man cannot have had anything to do with the attack. On the other hand, he knew that Elser was a member of the Red Front Fighters League, a group with close ties to the Communist Party, and he also knew about the incriminating objects that had been found on him. In Huber's view, the matter should be approached more from the angle of the motive. The man in front of him, who had now been interrogated for days, seemed to have a sensitive nature. Huber thought he had discovered a strong sense of justice in him. At least, his previous statements could convey that impression.

In preparation, Huber had read the transcripts of all the interrogations that had been performed up to that point. Perhaps this seemingly good-natured Elser had been persuaded to carry out the assassination by the ringleaders of the attack? He certainly had the necessary practical abilities, for he was a craftsman.

Huber wanted to proceed strategically on that afternoon of November 13, confronting Elser with his contradictory statements and relentlessly questioning him in those areas where he had so far hidden behind vague answers. At the same time, he wanted to appeal to his sense of moral values, provide him possible

41

"honorable" motives, thereby building him a bridge to confession. Carrot and stick—the time-tested method.

But Huber didn't get anywhere that day, either. Whenever he thought a question would make things difficult for Elser, the man fell silent or evaded him—particularly when he addressed his stay in Munich.

"So what were you living on here?" Huber asked. "You had no work at all."

Elser was silent for a long time. Finally, he said, "I had my savings. I looked for work. But it had to be right. Not just the pay . . ."

Huber had gotten used to answers like this. The man had nerves of steel. In a calm tone he stated his answers, and sometimes they even sounded plausible. But it was clear to Huber that the evidence argued against Elser's seemingly believable accounts.

All the details had long since been investigated. Among others, his former landlords had been questioned. Though Elser had told them he was looking for work, he could not name a single workshop where he had introduced himself during his stay in Munich. He had always rented properly with his real name and done nothing to make his landlords unhappy. On the contrary, they described him as a quiet tenant—a loner, yes, but helpful and friendly.

Frau Luchmann, with whom Elser had lived for a few weeks, remembered her calm, though occasionally somewhat odd-seeming, tenant.

He had a few heavy boxes with him. My husband helped him carry them to the cellar. Upstairs he kept only a wooden trunk, but it didn't fit into the small room, so we put it in the hallway. Herr Elser actually was a bit strange, but I didn't really notice that at the time. Only once did I open the door to his floor unannounced. He was crouching in front of his trunk and flipping through a folder of drawings. When he saw me, he threw everything back into the trunk and locked it.

And there was something else about her tenant that had struck Frau Luchmann: He always came home very late at night, and sometimes

42

he didn't come home at all. I noticed that when I went to bring him his breakfast. I was surprised, because he wasn't that type.

Others who had provided him accommodations were equally in the dark about what the quiet tenant did with his time. As long as he had not found a job, he was working on an invention, Elser told another landlady. Was this invention the "infernal machine" used later for the bomb attack?

Huber had visited the crime scene. The bomb had been built into the column on the gallery in front of which the Führer had spoken. Precise detective work had also yielded the conclusion that the explosive device had been positioned close to the floor— but that required prolonged work that could only have been done on the knees. At that moment, Huber remembered his reflections after the crime scene inspection. He stood up from his chair, walked around the large desk and instructed Elser to take off his pants. "Here, now . . . at once!"

Elser hesitated for a moment, seemingly embarrassed. "It's just about the knees," said Huber, planting himself in front of him.

Slowly Elser pulled up his pants legs, inch by inch . . . Huber saw immediately that his knees were swollen and inflamed. "Do you have something to say to me now?" he asked, breaking the silence.

Elser did not speak for a long time. Then, so softly that he could scarcely be heard, he asked, "If someone did something like that, what should he expect?"

Huber was surprised for a moment. Was that a confession? He answered, "That depends why he did it."

At that point, when the confession seemed to be mere minutes away, anyone else would have continued the interrogation, but Huber broke it off. "We'll see each other again later," he called to Elser without further explanation, as two officers escorted him to his cell. Huber was certain that he had proven Elser's guilt. The confession—the successful conclusion of his work—he wanted to stage dramatically that evening in the presence of the other leaders of the Bürgerbräu Attack Special Commission, Nebe and Lobbes.

Shortly before midnight, he had Elser brought to him again. Officers led him to a chair in front of the desk; behind it sat Huber. No one said a word, including Nebe and Lobbes, who were impatiently pacing, waiting for the confession. Elser seemed downcast and even smaller than usual. He kept drinking from the bottle of mineral water in front of him.

He looked around timidly. Then, without any prompting, he blurted it out: "Yes, I did it."

The Gestapo men looked at each other with relief. Elser reached for the bottle and filled his glass. He then recounted in detail how he had planned and built the bomb and planted it in the column. It was almost four o'clock in the morning when the transcriber wrote down Elser's last sentences. Afterward, he was brought back to his cell.

More often than on the previous nights, Gestapo guards observed him through the peephole. A dead assassin was of no use to anyone—least of all to the Nazi leadership.

* * *

In the interrogation room of the Wittelsbach Palace, Huber, Nebe, and Lobbes were at once relieved and pensive. The confession had triggered an avalanche of follow-up questions. How was it possible that a man could work undisturbed for nights on end on the gallery of the Bürgerbräu Beer Hall? Had there been no security measures before November 8?

According to Directive No. 34/36 of the Führer's deputy from March 9, 1936, the SS-Reichsführer or a senior SS officer appointed by him was solely responsible for all barriers and security measures at events in which Hitler participated. But here in Munich, the "old fighters" presided over a territory the SS and police could not infiltrate.

In November 1936, there had been a dispute between the Munich party leader Christian Weber and the city's chief of police Baron von Eberstein over the question of who was responsible for security at the event. At that time, Hitler had announced his decision: "At this gathering, my 'old fighters' will guard me under the leadership of Christian Weber. The responsibility of the police ends at the entrances to the hall." It had been handled the same way this time.

Inquiries had revealed that Josef Gerum, an old marcher and party member since 1920 who was a senior Gestapo officer in Munich, had assumed responsibility for security. In the summer of 1939, he had volunteered for army service and participated in the Polish campaign in a unit of the Geheime Feldpolizei (Secret Field Police). As he happened to be in Munich due to illness, he had been assigned on November 8 to take over security in the Bürgerbräu during Hitler's speech. The security measures had been cursory, confined to the patrolling of the hall. On the day of the event, security at the entrances was intensified and the participants observed. What could happen here among the old comrades-in-arms? After the attack, as Huber, Nebe, and Lobbes knew, the party leadership had been infuriated. All the blame was focused on Christian Weber, who now had to answer for the fact that he had entrusted a man like Gerum with such an important task.

On grounds of an alleged "danger of suppression of evidence," party comrade Gerum was even taken into custody for a short time. This made him extremely angry, and he threatened to complain to the Führer himself about this outrageous treatment. But the Gestapo investigators probably regarded it as possible that Gerum (who would later turn up in a note in Himmler's files as a malcontent and endlessly critical "old fighter type") was in cahoots with the assassins. In the meantime, Gerum had been released. They had a perpetrator. But who were the masterminds, the Gestapo men in the Wittelsbach Palace wondered. Who were the actual "string pullers"?

* * *

On the morning of November 14, Huber called his superior in Berlin, the chief of the Gestapo, SS-Oberführer Heinrich Müller. He was pleased to hear the news that Georg Elser had confessed. But at the end of the conversation, he asked the decisive question: "And who is behind it?"

Huber answered with consternation: "No one."

Annoyed, Müller shouted into the telephone: "Tell that to Himmler!"

The situation was awkward. Himmler had no use for a German craftsman who had raised his hand against the Führer of his own accord. He needed foreign manipulators, string pullers, a conspiracy of "world Jewry," the British, or Strasser. But Huber could not help with that.

In Berlin, there was great annoyance about the results of the Munich special commission—especially from Himmler. When he first set eyes on the interrogation transcripts from Munich, he wrote on them in his angular handwriting, *What idiot performed the interrogation?* The responsible men of the Bürgerbräu Attack Special Commission thus could not expect praise from Berlin; on the contrary, Himmler ordered a new investigation, this time under the exclusive control of the Gestapo. "Bring the perpetrator to Berlin," he commanded.

On the afternoon of November 14, Georg Elser was fetched from his cell. He looked tired; the nights of interrogations had worn him out. Almost drowsily, he asked, "What's going on? Am I going to be questioned again?"

A Gestapo officer laughed in his face. "My friend, now you're going to Berlin. There's a different climate there. You can talk more there."

Early that evening, Elser was transported to Berlin under heavy guard.

Not until seven days later, on November 21, did the German News Agency disseminate a "special report" on Elser's arrest.

Berlin, November 21—The SS-Reichsführer and chief of the German police announces: Immediately after the nefarious attack in the Bürgerbräu Beer Hall on November 8, 1939, measures were taken that seemed appropriate to solving the crime and facilitating the arrest of the perpetrator or perpetrators. In the course of this search operation, all German borders were immediately closed and border control was intensified.

Among those arrested that same night was a man who tried to cross the German border illegally into Switzerland. This was the thirty-six-year-old Georg Elser, most recently residing in Munich. The findings made in the meantime by the special commission sent to Munich by the security police yielded numerous clues to the preparation and execution of the deed.

By now at least some of the subjects connected to the crime have already been arrested. For further information the following questions are directed at the public:

- *Who knows Elser?*
- *Who can provide information on his circles?*
- *Who can identify people with whom Elser associates?*
- *Where has Elser been over the past several years?*
- *Where or from whom has he made purchases or placed orders?*
- *Who remembers Elser working on inventions, technical drawings, designs, etc.?*
- *Who has seen anyone else with drawings or plans of the Bürgerbräu Beer Hall?*
- *Who has seen Elser in restaurants, in train stations, on trains, on buses, etc., alone or with other people?*
- *Who has seen Elser outside the country? When, where, and with whom?*

Under the headline "The Munich Attack—The Most Horrible and Ingenious of All Crimes," the German News Agency disseminated another report. This one pulled out all the stops of National Socialist propaganda.

The interrogation of any criminal requires feeling out and getting to know his psychological substance. When the circle of suspicion had closed around Elser—when all his personal ties, his life's path, his associations were able to be precisely determined—it became possible in several further interrogations and confrontations to achieve certainty that the true perpetrator had been apprehended.

Under the weight of the evidence and the details that had since been secured in his places of refuge, the criminal's confession could ultimately only confirm the result of the investigation.

We have seen this man. He is the murderer of the victims of that terrible plan, the man who attempted to strike the Führer and with him the leadership of the Reich. One must repeatedly remind oneself of all this, for this man has no conspicuous criminal physiognomy, but intelligent eyes and a soft, deliberate manner of expression. The interrogations go on endlessly, he thinks long and hard about each word before he answers, and when one can observe him doing so, one forgets momentarily that one is standing before a satanic monster, whose conscience is capable of bearing so lightly such guilt, such a dreadful burden.

The history of crime knows no precedent for this most horrible and ingenious of all crimes. . . . In addition to the already available clear clues to the background of this disgraceful crime, the German public will now gather countless small pieces of information in conjunction with the security police, so that an unbroken, complete chain of evidence will be the undoing of everyone it implicates beyond any doubt.

In the meantime, not even the Propaganda Ministry could dispute Elser's guilt any longer, but the "chain of evidence" had to be pursued. No one needed a lone assassin, who on top of that had "no conspicuous criminal physiognomy" and even had "intelligent eyes." What they needed were masterminds. The official direction of the propagandistic exploitation of the attack had long been predetermined.

Seemingly by chance, the German Intelligence Service followed up that same day with a second "special report" on the arrest of two British secret service officers.

Berlin, November 21—The central office of the British Intelligence Service for Western Europe in The Hague has attempted for a long time to instigate plots in Germany and organize attacks or make contact with what they suspect are revolutionary organizations. Based on information from German emigrants that was as criminal as it was foolish, the British government and its Intelligence Service were of the opinion that an opposition existed in the state, in the party, and in the Wehrmacht with the goal of precipitating a revolution. In light of these circumstances, members of the security service of the SS were tasked with making contact with this British central office of terror and revolution in The Hague. In the belief that they were actually dealing with revolutionary German officers, the representatives of the British Intelligence Service revealed to them their intentions and plans, and in order to maintain ongoing contact with these supposed German officers, they even provided them with a special British radio transmitter and receiver by means of which the German Secret State Police has maintained contact with the British government to this day.

On November 9, the heads of the British Intelligence Service for Europe, Mr. Best and Captain Stevens, attempted to cross the Dutch border near Venlo into Germany. They were overpowered by the German border guards and delivered to the state police as prisoners.

A day after the attack in the Munich Bürgerbräu Beer Hall, two SS agents of the Reichssicherheitshauptamt (RSHA, Reich Security Main Office), Walter Schellenberg and Alfred Naujocks, posing as resistance fighters, had lured the two officers of the Secret Intelligence Service (SIS) into a trap. Near Venlo in the Netherlands, the two British men had been abducted and taken into Germany as prisoners.

The Munich attack was to be blamed on the British secret service in the time-tested manner, with the goal of an additional legitimization of the impending western offensive.

Until November 21, the arrest of Best and Stevens had been kept from the public, in anticipation of an especially "useful" date for propaganda purposes. Now, after Elser's confession, the right time seemed to have come.

Though the special report did not assert a connection between the arrested officers and Elser, the proximity in time and the nature of the report suggested just that. All that was missing was a liaison between the two, and there was no better candidate for that than Otto Strasser, whose Black Front activities directed against the Nazi regime were widely known. The only link between Elser and Strasser arose from the fact that Elser had attempted to escape to Switzerland and Otto Strasser was himself in Switzerland at that time. The propagandists swiftly constructed evidence that the British secret service was part of this plot as well.

An official announcement on November 23, 1939, declared that Strasser had departed for England "in a hurry" on the day after the attack. In reality, however, Strasser had not left Switzerland until November 13, and he had not gone to England but to France.

Strasser's decision to leave Switzerland had nothing to do with the attack. Due to his political activities, the Swiss authorities had not extended his residence permit, forcing Strasser to leave his place of exile.

But who was interested in the truth in those days? By depicting Elser as the instrument of his master Otto Strasser and implying the influence of the British secret service behind the scenes as the organizer and financial backer, the Nazi propagandists painted the picture of a conspiracy—with success.

The SS-Reichsführer and chief of the German police Heinrich Himmler had his officers summarize the results in another report on the internal political situation. On November 22, the "General Mood and Situation" was described as follows.

The apprehension of the Munich assassin was first announced to the public on Tuesday night via radio. The news was only made widely known by the newspapers on Wednesday morning. It made a tremendously strong impression on the public. Over the past few days, there had still been frequent discussion of the Munich attack among the public, stimulated in particular by the weekly newsreel in the movie theaters, though numerous rumors were also circulating, some of which contained nonsensical suspicions regarding the perpetrators. The announcement that has now been made of the result of the investigations carried out up to this point has had a very positive effect on the public mood, as far as could be determined so far. The disclosure that the organizer of the attack had been the British secret service and the news of the arrest of the members of the British secret service at the Dutch-German border have reinforced the hostile mood toward Great Britain, which had already been expressed in the past few days in the expectation of an imminent attack against England.

The same report noted approvingly that even the Catholic clergy had abandoned its refusal to take a position on the attack in light of the new results of the investigation. As evidence of this, the report quoted an article from the newspaper of the Archdiocese of Freiburg from November 19.

When such attacks succeed, whole peoples always bear the devastating consequences. Time and again, we learn that it was foreign powers at work. No wonder that when this abhorrent crime occurred, SS-Reichsführer Himmler declared that the tracks of the perpetrators led outside the country. . . . How much more the idea of God's providence imposes itself in this case, when the life of the Führer, the fate of the whole German people faced a profound threat at a moment of intense outward struggle for existence. Only thirty minutes earlier, Adolf Hitler himself had spoken the words: "We believe that what happens was intended by providence. . . . In grief the German people confronts the great misfortune of the dead and wounded, but in faith it turns to the Führer of its fate, whom providence so visibly protected."

The propaganda machine could not work better. Foreign powers were portrayed as the actual string pullers; the myth of providence protecting the Führer was invoked once again as confirmation that the fate of "the whole German people" was bound to him.

* * *

Georg Elser knew nothing of the role that the Nazi propagandists had assigned to him in the days after his confession. He knew nothing of the raids and arrests that had become everyday occurrences in his hometown of Königsbronn. Friends, acquaintances, neighbors, employers, and colleagues were all interrogated. He had no idea that his parents and siblings, as well as Elsa, his last long-term girlfriend, had been arrested and were sitting on a train to Berlin guarded by Gestapo officers.

He lay on the plank-bed and looked up at the cell window. Through the barred square he could see gray clouds rapidly drifting by. A sky with bars—all of Germany is one big prison, he thought. He heard muffled sounds from outside. He felt lonely.

CHAPTER SIX

Secret Gestapo Matter

Berlin, Prinz-Albrecht-Strasse 8. An address before which the Nazis' political opponents and the ideologically persecuted in Germany trembled. Here, in a former hotel building, all the threads of National Socialist terror converged. On September 27, 1939, Himmler had issued a decree ordering the merger of the Hauptamt Sicherheitspolizei (Main Office of the Security Police), which was a state organization, and the Sicherheitshauptamt (Security Main Office), which was a party organization. Now the most important organs of the Nazi politics of persecution, oppression, and extermination were concealed behind the collective name Reichssicherheitshauptamt (Reich Security Main Office). This was where the *Schreibtischtäter* (the "desk perpetrators," as they became known) worked. In a perverse mixture of bureaucratic procedure and unrestrained arbitrariness, they planned, organized, and controlled the National Socialist terror apparatus. It was they who chose the personnel of the Einsatzgruppen, special task forces whose mass executions claimed hundreds of thousands of victims. It was also staff members in this office who developed the gas van that was used for a period of time to murder Jews.

The protective custody department decided on internments in the concentration camps. Office IV, responsible for combating political opponents, was in charge of spying, arrest, life, and death. State officials as well as members of the party and the SS pursued their bloody work in the Reichssicherheitshauptamt.

Prinz-Albrecht-Strasse 8, the official address of the SS-Reichsführer and his staff, was the central site of the bureaucracy of tyranny.

By the late summer of 1933, the Gestapo had already built an "in-house prison" in the building. It was used primarily to confine prisoners who were to be interrogated there, largely serving as an internal detention center of the Gestapo's central office. As a decree from 1935 ambiguously put it, it was "police custody of a special sort."

Those brought to Prinz-Albrecht-Strasse had to fear for their lives. By all available means, Gestapo men sought to clear up suspicious affairs and uncover real or supposed resistance against the regime. They recoiled from no act of cruelty. When it was deemed necessary, the most brutal methods of torture were employed to find out connections, organizational networks, foreign contacts, or mere confidants.

In the early years, the torture took the form of terrible beatings. Prisoners were often beaten unconscious with sticks, belts, and whips. Later the torture was euphemistically designated "enhanced interrogation," bureaucratically regulated, and systematized. A report described a typical case.

> *The detained prisoner was brought to one of the offices on the top floor, which belonged to the departments that dealt with communists and social democrats. Here—and not in the basement—the interrogations and torture were carried out. The Gestapo officer asked a direct question, often introduced by some harmless remarks. If he did not receive the desired information, the prisoner was beaten by the interrogator himself or by summoned "assistants."*
>
> *The second round of questioning usually followed immediately. If the prisoner still could not or would not make a statement, another orgy of beatings ensued.*
>
> *If the prisoner was so battered that there was no way he could answer any longer, he was sent back to his cell, where he was often left for twenty-four hours without food and water and then once again interrogated, beaten, and tortured. For many prisoners, these abuses went on for weeks.*

Who were the inmates of the in-house prison, which in 1939 consisted of thirty-eight individual cells and one communal cell for about fifty prisoners? Where did they come from? In most cases, they were communists, social democrats, and unionists, as well as members of the socialist youth movement and smaller socialist parties and resistance organizations. Many of them came from Berlin, which, as the former stronghold of the labor movement, remained a center of resistance against National Socialism. On the other hand, the Gestapo had prisoners brought to Berlin from hundreds of miles away if the case in question had national significance. In those cases, special investigative commissions were formed, which subjected "their" prisoners in the building to incessant interrogations.

* * *

Georg Elser was one of those prisoners. His case was a secret Gestapo matter of a highly charged nature.

Himmler, who had personally taken on the case, could be pleased with the extent to which Nazi propaganda had so far been able to capitalize on the attack—but who was Georg Elser really? An inconspicuous craftsman? A strange outsider? A lone malcontent against the war, the Reich, and the Führer? Himmler granted his officers complete authority to find out the truth.

* * *

Waiting. Georg Elser sat on the wooden plank-bed in his cell and looked at the gray wall. You can't even stretch out your arms without hitting the walls, he thought. Walls wherever you reach. The cell—a musty, cramped rectangle, less than ninety square feet. In the back, a small window with bars, as big as two shoeboxes. At the foot of the bed, a massive wooden door with iron fittings and a peephole. Next to it, the toilet bucket, a stool, a small folding table. Over the previous days, he had left the cell only to shower. The guards had escorted him to a completely tiled room. Five showers, five washbasins, for more than fifty prisoners. The rest of the time, he sat in his cell and waited.

Elser sat waiting between four walls for the interrogations that took place daily, feeling as if he were hanging from invisible threads. His strength had diminished. The next day, the interrogations would continue. His head was teeming with questions—questions like snakes whose bites he knew were deadly. He found only simple answers, despite the danger.

Waiting. Evening had fallen. Elser heard the sounds of keys outside. Were they coming to take him to an interrogation at this hour? To lead him through a labyrinth of gated corridors, passing him from one guard to another, just as he had experienced daily since his arrival here in Berlin? No, the sounds ceased.

Elser still knew nothing of the role that the Nazi propagandists had publicly ascribed to him since his confession. He knew nothing of the raids and arrests in Königsbronn.

A few days after the attack, a veritable invasion of the Gestapo had befallen the tranquil village. In nearby Heidenheim, half a dozen officers were residing in the König Karl hotel and another four in the Hirsch hotel in Oberkochen. Every day, they came to Königsbronn, where they had converted the town hall into a gigantic interrogation center. Everyone had been questioned: the members of the zither club, the choir, the dance group, the hiking club, all Elser's friends and acquaintances, and especially his family members. And the interrogations were still in full swing—the Gestapo did not give up so easily.

On November 13, they had Elser's entire family arrested. His mother described the events years later.

> We were not told by the detectives why we were being taken. At the same time, our homes were searched, but we ourselves were not allowed to be present.
>
> Along with my husband and me, all our children were arrested: our daughters living in Stuttgart and in Schnaitheim, our daughter living in Königsbronn, and our son Leonhard. First we were brought to the Königsbronn town hall and held there for a while.
>
> In Königsbronn, we were not interrogated, but transported to Heidenheim, where we were locked up. We stayed in Heidenheim only until the evening of November 13, 1939. From there, we were taken to Stuttgart by car. There we were put in prison again, and we were divided. Each family member was confined separately. . . .

I no longer remember the name of the prison. I was put in a cell where there were another five women, while the rest of my family was in individual cells.

In Stuttgart, we remained in custody for about seven days, and I was not permitted to see my family during that time. I was questioned every day, often twice in one day. It was here that I first learned that my son was the assassin in the Bürgerbräu Beer Hall, and that this was the reason we had been locked up for seven days. . . .

The men also asked me about the course of my son Georg's life and wanted to know whether I knew anything about the attack, whether Georg had told us anything at home, with whom he was in contact, and similar things. During the interrogations, I stated that I had no idea about the attack, for it is in fact the case that my family and I knew nothing about this attack. Georg had never told us that he had such an intention. He never made such statements. I could not believe that Georg was supposed to be that assassin, for my heart had not thought he would do such a thing. . . .

After about seven days in the prison in Stuttgart, I was told that I was leaving that evening. A woman came to get me and accompanied me on the train to Berlin. I did not see my family then, either, and at the time, I did not know that they were brought to Berlin, too.

Leonhard Elser, Georg's younger brother by ten years, had heard about the Bürgerbräu attack over the radio. Among his colleagues in the Königsbronn ironworks, where he worked as a carpenter's assistant, it had been discussed only briefly. Even in Königsbronn, the remote village in the Swabian Alps, the National Socialists had rapidly gained popularity after coming to power in 1933; the local party group could not complain about a lack of members. The village cultural life, from the gymnastics club to the dance school, had long been "coordinated" under the Gleichschaltung policy. On holidays, swastika flags fluttered in the village streets. The prevailing conditions of Germany reigned in Königsbronn as well.

The ironworkers were rather reserved in their reactions to the report on the Munich assassination attempt on the Führer, particularly those who were not members of the party and who had retreated into silent inner emigration. One such worker was Leonhard Elser, a quiet young man of twenty-six who bore a striking resemblance to his brother Georg, was not especially interested in politics, and was happy to have a job. Fourteen months ago, he had married Erna, a pretty girl from the neighboring village of Itzelberg. She had just given birth to their first child, whom they named Erna. Now they lived in Leonhard's parents' house, upstairs in a small attic apartment. They had plans, wishes, longings—like all young couples.

On November 13, their tranquil everyday life was shaken. The director of the ironworks came to Leonhard's work area, which was unusual, and instructed the young man to come with him, telling him that two men from the Gestapo were in the office. Leonhard was taken aback. "Gestapo? What do they want from me?" In the office the two men showed their badges. Later Leonhard Elser stated:

> They told me to come with them. I wanted to change, but they did not allow it. In what I was wearing, blue overalls and a carpenter's apron, I was loaded into a car and brought to Stuttgart. I asked what was actually going on, but they didn't answer me. In Stuttgart, I was put in a prison, a sort of detention center in which there was nothing but political prisoners.
>
> I was locked in a cell with three other men. They then interrogated me several times. That was when I first found out that Georg was suspected of having planted the bomb against Hitler in Munich. Again and again, the Gestapo officers asked me whether I knew anything about it, whether Georg had told me anything about it. But I didn't know anything. I was completely surprised.

When Erna learned that her husband had been picked up by the Gestapo at work, she was extremely worried. Gestapo? What could they have wanted with Leonhard? She became even more distraught when she was told that Leonhard's parents, his sisters, and their husbands had been arrested, too. "For God's sake, what happened?" Erna asked. No one could give her an answer.

The following nights, Erna couldn't sleep. Her thoughts revolved anxiously around her husband Leonhard and his parents. What had they done? Why were they in prison in Stuttgart?

A few days later, when Erna was about to do the laundry, a car stopped in front of the house. Two men got out and approached the door to the laundry room, which was in an extension next to the house. "Are you Frau Elser?" one of the two officers asked tersely.

"Yes," she answered fearfully. The two men showed their badges. "Gestapo—pack your things and come with us. You're under arrest," one of them told her sharply.

She just barely found time to leave her little daughter in a neighbor's care with the request to inform her mother. Minutes later, she was sitting in the backseat of the car. The officers didn't say a word. Erna Elser felt her heart racing. She was afraid.

They drove to Stuttgart. The car stopped in the yard of the Gestapo prison on Büchsenstrasse. She was brought to the second floor. Hours of interrogation ensued. Only now did Leonhard's wife learn why she had been brought there.

"Did your brother-in-law Georg ever tell you of his intentions?" asked a stocky Gestapo officer in plainclothes.

"No," she answered, confused.

That evening, she was brought under guard to the main train station. On the platform, she was handed over to another plainclothes officer. The two of them boarded a train, the destination of which was unknown to her, and entered a compartment that had been reserved.

Behind drawn curtains waited an officer and a man she knew fleetingly by sight: Hermann Heller, a carpenter from Königsbronn. Her brother-in-law Georg had lived for a period of time as a tenant in Heller's house. After he had discovered that Georg was having an affair with his wife, he had kicked him out. Later, he and his wife had gotten a divorce. Whether that was only because of the episode with Georg, Erna didn't know. Now they were sitting silently opposite each other. The officers had forbidden them to converse.

Erna thought of her little daughter and of Leonhard, whom she had not seen for days. She could not know that he was sitting under guard not many yards from her in another compartment, nor could she know that her parents-in-law, her sisters-in-law, and their husbands—indeed, the whole Elser family—had been brought together on this train by the Gestapo. The destination was Berlin, the Reichssicherheitshauptamt.

Each of them felt isolated; none of them knew about the presence of the others. In the rearmost compartment of the special car sat a young woman who was not a member of the Elser family, but from whom the Gestapo officers in Berlin were nonetheless hoping for valuable testimony. Her name was Elsa, and she had formerly been the wife of Hermann Heller and, for a long time, the lover of Georg Elser.

The last time they had seen each other had been in January 1939 in Stuttgart, where Georg had stayed with his sister for a few days. They had gone for a stroll together. *He told me that he wanted to move to Munich to look for work,* she later testified. *Earlier we had always talked about getting married, but after we did not come to an agreement at this meeting, and I noticed that the thought of marriage was far from his mind, I explained to him that I would not go along with this uncertainty much longer and would get married as soon as I found an honest man.*

The end of her hopes was also the end of her love for Georg. That summer, she met Karl, who worked in the same Esslingen factory as she did—a decent, humble, and faithful man, with firm marriage intentions. During that time, she received only two brief letters from Georg, in which he informed her that he had found a nice room and a small workshop where he could do carpentry work in Munich.

She wrote back to him and asked where he was working, what he was doing, and how much he was earning, but she did not receive an answer. After that, she came to a final decision: He would remain a fond memory, but nothing more. She wanted to get married again. The date for her wedding to Karl had already been set.

Then came that Wednesday. In the office, she had spoken to colleagues about the attack, and Irmgard, her colleague and friend, mentioned that an assassin had been arrested—a certain Elster or something like that. For a moment she was taken aback by the name, intuitively, a reflex. Georg was living in Munich . . . but an assassin? No, he could not be the perpetrator.

Later, she stated:

When I arrived in Jebenhausen, on Wednesday, my mother told me that Georg had committed the attack and his whole family had been arrested. There I saw his picture in the newspaper for the first time. I had been home for barely half an hour when I was arrested by a detective from Göppingen in my mother's apartment and immediately brought to the Stuttgart police headquarters. He treated me like a criminal and did not even give me the chance to take along a handkerchief, much less toiletries. In Stuttgart, I was not interrogated, but only held in custody on Büchsenstrasse until evening. That same evening, I was brought to the main train station.

Now she thought back to the time with Georg. He was a quiet man—someone who knew nothing but carpentry and his passion for music, someone who always said exactly what he meant. He did not like chatter or debates. He was opposed to the Nazis, about whom he had nothing positive to say. Once, when they were sitting in a restaurant, a man in SA uniform had come in and had passed around a collecting box. She could not recall what it was for, but she remembered well that Georg was annoyed when she inserted a small donation. "Either you are for them, and you give something, or you are against them, and you give nothing," he said reprovingly.

The train moved through the night. Early the next morning, she would be in Berlin. She imagined traveling without the two Gestapo officers—with Karl . . . on their honeymoon. To Berlin, the city of which she had so often dreamed. The large boulevards, the fancy shops, the beautiful cafés . . . now she was on the way to this colorful dream world, but she wanted nothing more than to turn back. Now she was afraid of the city. Would she be confronted with Georg? What did they actually want from her?

* * *

Georg Elser waited for morning. Freezing, he went to the cell window, which was ajar, and closed it. Dank, stuffy air remained in the cell. Later he rolled from side to side, unable to sleep.

61

He could not get used to the hard, wooden bed and the worn-out mattress. He stood up and paced the narrow cell. He saw through the window the beam of the large searchlight, which cast a long shadow of the window bars on the bare gray wall. If only the nights were not so long, he thought. What to do with the loneliness, the fear?

Guilt, despair, and powerlessness deprived him of sleep. He imagined how unhappy his mother must be, his siblings and their families. Undoubtedly, the Gestapo had made things difficult for them and interrogated them. He thought of his friend Eugen. Elser had once hinted to him that the Hitler regime should be abolished. He hoped that he had kept that to himself and had not put himself in danger. Eugen, his friend, with whom he had played as a child, who had sat next to him in school, had roamed with him through the fields in the afternoon, and later, in the traditional costume society, had looked for young women with him. Eugen, who had recently gotten married and still lived in Königsbronn—how might he be doing?

More and more often, images from the past had been creeping up on Elser during the past several nights—from his childhood and youth in Königsbronn.

CHAPTER SEVEN

Königsbronn Years

High up in the mountains of eastern Württemberg, where the people's lives are marked by frugality and modesty, Georg Elser was born on January 4, 1903, in the small village of Hermaringen.

His mother, Maria Müller, a twenty-four-year-old woman, lived in her parents' house. They ran a wagon-making and repair shop. Not until a year after Georg's birth did she marry his father, Ludwig Elser, a farmer's son who was seven years older than she was. He came from nearby Ochsenberg, where he had grown up with eighteen siblings. From an early age, Ludwig had been required to lend a hand on his parents' farm. After school, he and his older siblings began the actual daily work, consisting of arduous tasks in the barn and fields that often lasted until late in the evening. Despite a hard, deprived childhood and youth, Ludwig had been spared illnesses and had grown to independence as a tough, somewhat taciturn-seeming young man—a farm boy who had found the right woman in Maria.

In November 1904, shortly after the wedding, the young couple moved with little Georg to Königsbronn, not many miles from Hermaringen. There Ludwig bought his own land with an inheritance and started a lumber trade. On the side, the couple ran a modest farm. Maria bore the brunt of the farming work, and that did not change when a second child, their daughter Friederike, was born on October 19, 1904. Maria was a mother, housewife, and farmer from early in the morning to the late

63

evening hours, day after day. She fulfilled her duties as she had always done in her parents' house: humbly and meekly. Two years later, she had a third child, another girl. She was named Maria.

Georg, by then three and a half years old, was a rather quiet, small child. For hours, he would sit in the garden next to the house and keep himself occupied or play with his younger sister Friederike in the sandbox. Quarrels were rare. He especially enjoyed family visits with his grandparents in Hermaringen. There was soda and cake, sometimes even a piece of fried sausage, and—best of all—his parents forgot for a few hours their hard everyday life and played with him and Friederike. His mother in particular savored the few free Sundays.

Shortly before Georg was to start school, a fourth child was born on May 21, 1909. His brother Ludwig was granted only a short life, though, as less than six years later, on January 4, 1915, he died of lung disease. On October 10, 1910, Anna came into the world, and three years later, on June 1, 1913, another boy was born, who was given the name Leonhard.

The Elsers were now a large family. Though this was not out of the ordinary in those days, there were nonetheless many mouths to feed. The father's lumber trade was not doing especially well, and the small farm, which still rested on the mother's shoulders, brought in only modest sums. From a very early age, Georg had to help in the barn, in the fields, and in the house. And, as the oldest, he always had to look after his younger siblings.

But it was not only the family's financial situation that was precarious; there were also repeated marital disputes, which frequently led to physical confrontations. The father began to drown his problems in alcohol, which made him violent and aggressive.

Later Georg remembered this oppressive period of his childhood.

Not every day, but often, my father came home very late. As far as I know, he was often in the tavern. My mother told us children that my father often hit her, though I didn't see this happen. Whether my father hit my mother only with his hand or with a chair, a lamp, or with something else, I don't know. Sometimes when he came home at night, our father got us out of bed for some reason—for example, to take off his boots—but I can't remember him ever hitting us at night when he was drunk, and I don't think that happened. From my father, I often got beatings when I had done something wrong. From my mother, too, I occasionally—not often—got beatings. We always woke up at night when my father came home drunk. When he entered the house, he was always ranting. It was not the case that my father was drunk, say, only on Saturdays, but it also occurred on weekdays, at all different times. As far as I know, he drank only beer and wine. Not much liquor, I think. I don't remember ever hearing my father promise my mother to stop drinking.

For a long time, Maria Elser put up with her husband's outbursts. But once, in the summer of 1910, after her husband had once again hit her during a quarrel, she left the house with the children for a week. *During that week she stayed with us children at her parents' house in Hermaringen,* Georg later recalled. *One of my father's sisters persuaded my mother to return to Königsbronn.*

That same year, Georg started school in Königsbronn. He was an average student; only in the subjects that particularly interested him—such as drawing, arithmetic, and penmanship—did he receive good grades. In drawing class, he got attention for making funny little pictures, in which he gave his teachers and schoolmates humorous speech balloons. During one class, the teacher caught him coloring one of his funny pictures alongside the actual drawing assignment. "Georg," he called sternly, "come here and bring your drawing with you . . ." With his head lowered, little Georg stood up amid the smirks of his classmates and slunk to the desk at the front of the room. Everyone was expecting a scolding. The teacher, a round man with a narrow mustache, cast a glance at the paper. Then his face lit up. "You have imagination—and a good hand . . ." He confiscated the little pictures and sent Georg back to his seat. The boy was as pleased with the lack of punishment as he was with the public praise. In the fourth grade, his talents were recognized once again. The teacher gave him a sketchbook for his achievements in drawing. Georg was very proud of that. For a long time, he hesitated to draw in the book he had received as a gift.

His parents, however, were only moderately interested in their child's schoolwork. Later Georg commented on that in an interrogation transcript: *As far as I can remember, my parents were not very concerned with the report cards I brought home from school. I can't remember them ever asking me whether I got good or bad grades, though both of them always helped me a bit with homework. Because I had to assist with the farming work at home, studying was difficult for me.*

It was not that important to his father for Georg to be a good student. It was enough for him to know that he was not one of the bad ones. He just didn't want Georg to have to repeat a year. Georg was slated to work for his father and one day take over the lumber trade. For that, he didn't need model grades, his father thought. Georg should learn how to work with his hands—and the earlier, the better.

In the spring of 1917, having just turned fourteen, Georg finished primary school. His final report card was average. Only in his favorite subjects, drawing and arithmetic, were his grades good. Until autumn, he somewhat reluctantly helped his father transport lumber, which was strenuous work, ten hours a day, rain or shine. On the weekend, he supported his mother on the farm, where he mainly worked in the fields and fed the livestock in the barn.

He was not paid for his work. For his parents, it went without saying that their oldest son would not demand that. But Georg found it unjust that he also had to do without pocket money. At least a few marks like others his age in the village—was that too much to ask? On Sunday, the only free day of the week, he could not afford a soda with his companions. That embarrassed him, so he preferred just to stay home. On Monday, the torture began anew, and he accepted it without complaints.

When Georg mentioned one evening that he wanted to apply for an apprenticeship as a lathe operator in the ironworks, his father reacted gruffly. "What do you want with that?" he shouted. "I need you. You're going to take over the business." But Georg was not impressed by his father's loud words. He had set his mind on doing an apprenticeship as a lathe operator, just like his friend Eugen. During his interrogations, he described how his decision had ripened.

I got the idea of becoming a lathe operator because my schoolmate Eugen began an apprenticeship in an ironworks immediately after graduation. It was not that he described this job to me in especially glowing terms or brought me pieces he had worked on, but the mere fact that my friend was a lathe operator led me, without my knowing exactly why, to take up this job, too.

My father's occupation and farm work had never appealed to me. I had worked on the farm less out of pleasure in the work than out of the desire to help my mother. Dealing with horses did not much suit me, and on top of that I had witnessed how various horses had died, which also spoiled my pleasure in transporting lumber.

Despite his father's reproaches and complaints that he was losing an important worker, Georg stuck to his decision. With his mother's support, he got the apprenticeship and began training to be a lathe operator in the autumn of 1917. In the factory were two foremen, as many as forty workers, and four other apprentices in addition to Georg. The work was done in two shifts. Later, Georg described his apprenticeship.

In the first three months of my employment in the ironworks, I had to assist the older lathe operators by bringing tools for repair, fetching material, etc. I could not perform any work on my own. At the end of the first three months, I began working on my own at a small lathe under the supervision of the foreman. I had to cut threads, tighten bolts, grind anvils, and perform other, smaller lathe operations. After some time, I began working at a larger lathe, because my model was too light, especially for grinding anvils. In the period that followed, I did somewhat more difficult lathe work.

In the factory, there was often heavy iron dust. In the rear area, iron was heated, and from there warm air permeated the floor. After a few months, Georg noticed that the work did not agree with his health. He complained of headaches and nausea, and often had fevers. Several times he consulted a doctor, who was unable to help him.

At the end of February 1919, he went to the factory office and declared that he wanted to break from his apprenticeship, because he could not tolerate the work. Fourteen days later, he left the ironworks. He was sad to no longer to be able to spend lunch breaks with his friend Eugen and attend the vocational school in nearby Heidenheim, where he had been among the better students in the lathe operating class. On the other hand, it had become clear to him shortly after the beginning of his apprenticeship that he would rather work with wood than iron.

At home, he had amassed a modest tool collection, for which his father had given him money. Otherwise, he had to pay his dues. He was not allowed to keep anything, and he was still not granted an allowance. So what else was there for him to do but spend his Sundays working with wood?

Georg built rabbit hutches, carpentered small bookshelves, and repaired damaged furniture. The decision to give a carpentry apprenticeship a try was thus a natural next step. During his apprenticeship in the ironworks, Georg had made the acquaintance of the master carpenter Sapper, whose workshop was close to his parents' house. At the behest of his father, he often fetched sawdust and wood chips there, which were used as litter for the barn. There he watched the journeymen at work, which further aroused his interest in carpentry.

On March 15, 1919, Georg began his new apprenticeship. Regarding the work there, he later commented: *In the early period of my work I had to make simple boxes, stools, and things like that, which demanded no special skills at all. I had to cut wood to size, plane it, and assemble it. The tasks got progressively harder, and at the end of my apprenticeship I was able to make large and heavy furniture on my own. I took great pleasure and great interest in that work.*

Architectural carpentry, which was part of the job, too, appealed less to Georg. He didn't like the dirt and dust of that coarse work. He preferred the fastidious craftsmanship of cabinetmaking. That was also where he received praise from his master.

Georg was recognized as an extraordinarily talented furniture maker, equally strong in design and construction. Despite his good work, however, the apprentice's wages were meager. In the first year of the apprenticeship, he received one reichsmark per week; in the second, two; and in the third, four. In the meantime, his parents had stopped withholding the low pay. Georg spent some of the money on clothing, but mainly he purchased carpentry and metalworking tools, such as planes, drills, and files, and set up a small home workshop in his parents' basement.

Georg was an eager apprentice. He gave no cause for criticism, scrupulously finishing all his tasks and rarely, if ever, missing a day of work. In the spring of 1922, he passed the journeyman's exam at the Heidenheim vocational school at the top of his class. Everyone was pleased: the master, the journeymen, and even his father. Georg was happy; he had achieved his goal and, for the first time in his life, felt truly appreciated.

Until that December, he remained in his apprenticeship workshop as a journeyman. He then gave notice in order to go work in the Rieger furniture factory in Aalen. The master, who relied on Georg's outstanding handicraft skills, rejected his resignation. In early 1923, he resubmitted his resignation, which did not meet with the master's approval that time, either. Then Georg stopped going to work. Fourteen days later, he began his job as a cabinetmaker in Aalen, where his primary occupation was making kitchen and bedroom furniture.

He kept his room in his parents' house. Every day he took the train early in the morning from Königsbronn to Aalen, and often he did not return until late in the evening. *I didn't make any friendships with my colleagues,* he recalled later. *In my free time, I did incidental repairs at home. I no longer had time to make things.*

Georg's life consisted mainly of work. Only on Sunday was there time to unwind. That was when he would meet Eugen, his best friend. He trusted him and felt comfortable enough with him to speak his mind. Among other things, he talked to him about quitting his job. "My work isn't paid properly. You do your work, and the money is worthless. I'd rather quit."

In the autumn of 1923, he quit. The decision wasn't easy for him, but unlike many of his colleagues who shared his fate, he accepted the consequences of the rising inflation. They were hard, drastic consequences, which included returning to work on his parents' farm. Later he recalled that period.

I helped my mother as I had earlier with the work in the fields and assisted my father, who had been carrying on the lumber trade, with logging work, such as trimming, sawing, chopping, and things like that. I did not receive any compensation or allowance from my mother or father. I had room and board at home. In those days, I spent my free time with my friend Eugen, who had a gramophone at home and taught me how to dance. I didn't do much woodworking at that time. Until the summer of 1924, I worked at home in the way I've described.

Around that time, he inquired again about work at a carpenter's workshop in Heidenheim. Based on his good credentials, he was hired three days later, which was welcome news for him, because the few months at home had shown him that he could no longer work with his father, whose outbursts afflicted him. Despite the fact that he was now twenty-one years old, his father still ordered him around like a young boy.

In Heidenheim, too, he performed his work to the full satisfaction of his master. The slim journeyman, who built wardrobes and kitchen furniture in the sawdust-covered wood workshop, was known after a short time as an especially capable worker. His colleagues appreciated his quiet, humble manner.

They were thus all the more disappointed when Georg gave notice to the owner in January 1925 because he wanted to move away. The decision to quit his job again had nothing to do with the conditions at his workplace. Though he sometimes worried that he could not sufficiently perfect his technical ability there and did not often feel challenged in his craft, his decision was an expression of more basic considerations.

He had become aware in recent weeks that he found life in Königsbronn constricting, paralyzing, and depressing. He felt demoralized by the irascible, unrestrained behavior of his father, who increasingly suffered from alcoholism; the lamentable situation of his mother, who could not protect herself from her husband's attacks and for whom he felt sympathy without being able to do anything to help her; and the superficial, distant relationships with his siblings, who did not share his interests any more than he did theirs.

My brother had a somewhat unique character. He was taciturn and did not have much to do with us siblings, but always went his own way. Thus his sister Maria characterized him later. And Leonhard, his younger brother by ten years, recalled, *As a child, and later on, too, I didn't get along especially well with my brother Georg.*

Georg had a taciturn and reserved nature. He didn't talk much and avoided debates, whatever the topic. He made few close friends among his schoolmates and later among his colleagues. A rather quiet, sensitive, musical type, he played the flute and accordion in school and later performed as an entertainer for small groups. He was well liked. He was especially popular with girls, because he was not a loud reveler like the other boys.

Georg was a loner, maintaining close contact only with Eugen, his childhood friend. On Sundays, they would go on walks together from Königsbronn, and he would speak to Eugen about his worries, problems, and plans. "I think I'll travel," he told him one February Sunday on the way to Oberkochen, about four miles away. "You know," he went on, "I don't really feel content here in Königsbronn."

In this remark, Eugen thought he heard melancholy and disappointment more than excitement for a journey. Eugen suspected what was making Georg so despondent: his father's constant outbursts, his alcoholism—and perhaps, he thought, it was also the stark contrast between the peaceful rural idyll and the stressful, hectic life in his parents' house that aroused Georg's desire to move away. Was his departure an escape? An attempt to find an orderly life in a new place?

Eugen was uncertain. Should he be happy or sad about his friend's plans? He would miss Georg—their walks, their conversations, the things they did together, his music, his advice, and his courage.

CHAPTER EIGHT

Departure

On February 26, 1924, an edition of the *Völkischer Beobachter* appeared again for the first time since the newspaper had been banned after the Hitler putsch, announcing for the following day a meeting of the National Socialists in the Bürgerbräu Beer Hall—the site of the failed coup. "A New Beginning," read the headline under the newspaper's logo, in which the words *Freiheit und Brot* (Freedom and Bread) were now written in small print above the eagle with the swastika, the registered emblem of the Nazi Party. *Herausgeber Adolf Hitler* (Publisher Adolf Hitler) was written under the title. The *Völkischer Beobachter*—purchased from the Thule Society, a "Germanic order," in December 1920 by Hitler and his backers (probably from the Reichswehr) for 120,000 *Papiermarks*—had been banned immediately after the putsch on November 9, 1923. By then, the National Socialist mouthpiece, appearing in an unusual six-column broadsheet format, had a circulation of 30,000 copies per day.

Until 1922, Hitler had written many leading articles; thereafter, he had his speeches published in the newspaper. His early articles were already hate-filled appeals to his followers' will to combat. In the March 6, 1922, edition, he wrote:

> *We will rouse the people. And not only rouse them, we will whip them up. We will preach battle, relentless battle against this whole parliamentary brood, this whole system, which will not cease until Germany is either*

destroyed or one day some iron skull comes, perhaps with dirty boots, but with a clear conscience and a steel fist, who will end the chatter of these parquet heroes and give the nation a deed.

Now, on February 27, 1925, the Nazi Party, which was itself banned after the November putsch, was to be reestablished under the same name. Hitler had already been released on December 20, 1924, from his prison term, which he later referred to with amusement as a "university at state expense." The remainder of the sentence from which he had been pardoned was officially noted: *3 years, 333 days, 21 hours, 50 minutes.* At the request of the state prosecutor at the Munich Regional Court I, the prison warden had written a report describing Hitler as an exemplary prisoner.

Hitler has shown himself to be a man of order and discipline, not only with respect to himself, but also with respect to his fellow inmates. He is content, humble, and agreeable. Makes no demands, is quiet and reasonable, serious and without any abusive behavior, tries painstakingly to comply with the prison restrictions. He is a man without personal vanity, is satisfied with the institution's food, does not smoke or drink, and, while comradely, is able to secure a certain authority over his fellow inmates. . . . Hitler will seek to reignite the national movement according to his principles, however no longer by violent means, if necessary directed against the government, but in contact with the proper government authorities.

On December 20, a telegram arrived from Munich, in which the regional court judge ordered Hitler's immediate release. Thus his term in the Landsberg Prison had ended. He had been able to spend it in the circle of his followers without any hardship. He ate his daily meals together with them in a large common room in which a swastika flag adorned the wall. Fellow inmates kept his cell in order, handled his correspondence, and reported to the Führer each morning. Life in fortress confinement was reminiscent of the atmosphere in an officers' club, as the prisoners ordered their favorite meals from the prison guards, smoked, played cards, and could receive visits from the outside as they pleased. There were days when Hitler, who was actually entitled to only six visiting hours per week, received over twenty guests in succession in the "fortress parlor" set up specifically for those meetings.

Hitler also regularly went for walks in the institution's garden, accompanied by numerous loyalists. And in the evening, when he spoke to his comrades about his ideas and visions, even the prison officials listened, silent and motionless with admiration, to his words.

Hitler used the prison term, which forced him to take a breather from his public political activities, to set down in writing the foundations of his ideological system. Rudolf Hess spent hours hammering Hitler's worldview into the typewriter. In his writings, he put down on paper what would become a rigorous program after his release: the confessional work *Mein Kampf*, the first volume of which appeared in 1925 under the title *Eine Abrechnung* (*A Reckoning*).

At the event in February 1925 at the Bürgerbräu Beer Hall, the first since his release, Hitler now wanted to gather the countless— occasionally factionalized and competing—nationalist groups and associations in order to present his political goals, visions, and plans. Though the event did not begin until eight o'clock in the evening, audience members were already streaming into the hall in the early afternoon. Two hours before it began, the doors had to be closed. Roughly 4,000 supporters waited expectantly for Hitler. When he finally entered the hall, cheers burst out.

In a two-hour speech, Hitler urged the crowd to forget the past, settle differences, bury hostilities, and under his leadership take German history into their hands. "World Jewry" had to be combated, Marxism toppled. A new beginning was imminent, a new national movement.

Hitler sent his audience into a frenzy of joy. The disgrace of 1923 was forgotten; now there was nowhere to go but "forward." Was this the breakthrough?

* * *

Less than 200 miles away, in the remote village of Oberkochen, life continued on its leisurely course. It was Sunday. In the Zum Hirsch tavern, Georg and Eugen sat with a quarter-liter bottle of wine and waited for Friedel. Certainly—here in the rural idyll, too— there were nationalist undercurrents, the bogeyman of Marxism could stoke people's fears, and enemies could be demonized through propaganda. But here there was no trace of a "national movement" as in Munich. Politics was not an issue. That was the case for Georg and Eugen, too. They talked about their plans, their dreams—rarely, if ever, about politics.

In recent months, the two of them had often trekked over from Königsbronn, even when cold and snow made the route arduous. They enjoyed the vastness of the natural landscape, which aroused in them a strange mixture of emotions: the feeling of being at home and the longing to set off on a journey.

They were regulars at the Hirsch. The tavern keeper was a friendly man with a round figure, who brought good inexpensive food to the table and always had time for a chat with his guests. Here Georg had made the acquaintance of Friedel, a robust young fellow from Oberkochen, who was also a carpenter by trade. He had told him about his intention of moving away, and Friedel had given him the address of a master carpenter in Bernried, a small village near Lake Constance, where he himself had once found work during his travels.

"You'll learn a lot there," Friedel had told him. "Every master has his own craft, his own style."

Shortly thereafter, Georg had applied and been accepted. *You can begin working for me as a journeyman. I will expect you on March 15*, wrote the master carpenter only five days later. On that Sunday, Georg raised his glass to Friedel and Eugen: "To a good journey!"

On March 14, he took the train to Tettnang and then walked more than two hours to Bernried. After his arrival, he found out that he was the only journeyman. He was disappointed with the work, too; as in earlier workshops, his job was to make furniture, but here, aside from a self-made circular saw, there were no machines at all. Even the planing work had to be done by hand.

It quickly became clear to Georg that there was no opportunity for further training. Nor did he like the village. Bernried consisted of only a few houses, so that he soon felt quite lonely. In May he quit and, without the prospect of a steady job, continued on his wanderings. Later he recalled those first weeks in a strange place.

I trekked through Langenarden along Lake Constance toward Friedrichshafen and Manzell. From Bernried to Friedrichshaften, I walked for about a week. I spent the nights at inns and along the way asked repeatedly for work to no avail. On this journey, I was always alone. I didn't beg or peddle then or later. I paid the inn bills from my savings. From the employment agency in Friedrichshafen, where I inquired, I learned that the Dornier factory in Manzell was looking for a skilled carpenter. I took the job and was employed in propeller construction. About fifteen to twenty people worked in this department. Because I couldn't get a room in the immediate vicinity of the factory due to the tourist season, I rented lodgings in Kluftern, a town on the railroad line between Manzell and Markdorf. I took the train every day back and forth between Manzell and Kluftern. In Kluftern I stayed at an inn, the name of which I can't remember. In this job I earned quite good wages through piecework and a lot of overtime hours—more than ever before, anyway.

At that time, Georg became friends with Leo, a young fellow who worked as a carpenter for the same company. The two of them had something else in common as well: Leo, too, liked to play music.

On warm Sundays, they would sometimes take the train to Friedrichshafen or Konstanz, hike along the lake, and stop at one of the inns on the way. One evening, after their return, Leo took out his clarinet and gave a small private concert for Georg. "Let's go to Konstanz together," Leo proposed. "There we can play in the dance orchestra of the traditional costume society—you with your accordion, I with my clarinet; that would be something . . . They could really use us."

Georg, who was always somewhat reserved about presenting his musical abilities in public, shook his head. "But how will we get to the orchestra rehearsals?" he asked thoughtfully. "For that we'd have to go to Konstanz."

Leo laughed. "Well, then let's look for a new job there!"

In the days that followed, they talked often about quitting their well-paid jobs and going to Konstanz together. In August, the time had finally come; Leo had persuaded Georg. They gave notice and took a boat from Friedrichshafen to Konstanz. It was the first boat ride of Georg's life. He felt as if he were crossing the Atlantic. The lake seemed endless to him. Far away on the horizon, the clouds darkened and sank into the lake. Georg thought of Königsbronn, his mother, and Eugen. He planned to send them a postcard from Konstanz.

After a few days, the two men were hired as carpenters in a clock factory. The company sold finished grandfather clocks and produced the cases for them. The work was varied and to Georg's liking. He stayed with this company until the end of 1929, but due to lack of orders there were several changes of ownership and even a bankruptcy. For him, this meant multiple interruptions, at times for a few weeks and once even for half a year.

Georg shared the fate of many colleagues. For months he lived off unemployment benefits and his savings. It ran counter to his worldview to take each day as it came without work. He, who had been accustomed to working from his early youth onward, who loved his craft, who in fact based his whole identity on his work, suffered from this condition.

In early 1929, when after a few months the production of the company, which was now called Upper Rhenish Clock Manufacturing, was stopped once again, Georg worked for half a year as a cabinetmaker in Switzerland. In Bottighofen, a small village six miles south of Konstanz, he had found another job through a newspaper ad.

For an hourly wage of 1.30 Swiss francs, the equivalent of 1.04 reichsmarks, Georg built furniture. Early in the morning he rode his bike from Konstanz, where he had rented a room, across the border to Bottighofen. He had his bike tagged at the customs office, got a pass for "local border traffic," and was thus able to cross the border without inspections. Though he had at one point considered renting a small apartment in Switzerland, he ended up staying in Konstanz after all, where he had found something like a second home in recent years. In the meantime, he had lost close contact with Leo, but had found new acquaintances.

Georg had meanwhile become a valued member not only in the orchestra of the traditional costume society, where he had become an indispensable player due to his musical talent, but also among the Konstanz Friends of Nature. There, among politically like-minded people, he felt comfortable. Nonetheless, he was reserved with his opinions. He was not a man of many words; occasionally he made a brief remark regarding political issues, but that was as far as it went. People who were more closely acquainted with him knew that Georg had two sides. On the one hand, he was a quiet, taciturn man, who seemed reticent, sometimes downright shy. On the other hand, there was the gregarious, even entertaining Georg. He loved to be in the company of others; he just didn't want to be the center of attention. He offered his help everywhere, especially where he could make use of his handicraft skills.

His humble behavior and his attractive appearance won him a lot of sympathy among the young female members of the society in particular. Georg was so different from the rest of the young men, for he barely drank, didn't show off, and was extremely charming. In his time in Konstanz, he was a desired lover. *I had met several young women in a row there, so that my time was full. Some of them I saw for a longer period,* he recalled later.

The relationship with one of these women was not without consequences. Mathilde, his girlfriend, got pregnant. The two of them were not happy about it. How would they find an apartment? How would Georg, who had so often been without work recently, feed a family of three? And did they even want to get married? They liked each other, of course—they were in love. But was that enough for a marriage? Mathilde and Georg spent many evenings talking about their situation and their future. He later testified about what ensued.

At the time when we thought she was in the second month of pregnancy, we were given an address in Geneva where it would be terminated. We went together, Mathilde and I, to Geneva. Mathilde was examined, and it was determined that she was already in the fourth month, and an intervention could no longer be made. A woman had performed the examination. We did not have to pay anything for it. We stayed the night in Geneva and went back to Konstanz the next day. I paid the travel costs.

The child was born, a boy, who was given the name Manfred.

Months later, the relationship with Mathilde began to dissolve. They were no longer getting along. They had to admit to themselves that it had been a brief, stormy affair and nothing more. Georg saw his son often up to the age of six months, but not after that. In the period that followed, everything he earned in excess of 24 reichsmarks was deducted from his weekly wages as alimony.

Georg was not exactly happy with this arrangement, but he accepted it. "One day I will take custody of the boy, and my mother will take care of him," he told himself in order to soothe his conscience. But he soon realized that such thoughts arose only from his guilt. And he knew: Manfred belonged to Mathilde. He was her child.

Later Georg would no longer have long-term relationships with women—perhaps that was partly because, as a result of the alimony payments for his illegitimate child, he was not financially capable of starting his own family. An intact, harmonious family, entirely different from what he had experienced—that would always remain a distant longing for Georg. And his family? He had written a few times to his mother; he had sent his brother Leonhard a card from an excursion on Lake Constance; he had gone to Königsbronn twice in recent years. Home had not changed much. His father was still drinking, and his mother continued to bear her fate with resignation. On the way back, a sad mood had overcome Georg. The circumstances in his parents' house still depressed him.

In early 1930, while on a stroll, he ran into a former colleague from the Konstanz clock factory and learned from her that one of the earlier partners in the company was now producing clock cases again in Meersburg. The next day, Georg went there and inquired about work. A few days later, he received a letter of acceptance to begin as a carpenter. Georg was relieved. The work in Switzerland in the small family business had not satisfied him. He had not felt challenged in his craft.

Georg now took the ferry daily across the lake to Meersburg and worked from seven in the morning until six in the evening. After work, he returned to Konstanz, where he had rented a new room on Fürstenbergstrasse. Aside from rehearsal evenings with the orchestra and occasional meetings of the Friends of Nature, he spent his free time exclusively with Hilda, a young waitress he had befriended. Georg built her a small sewing table and invited her on boat rides on Lake Constance. On Sundays, they took long walks.

Georg was in love with Hilda. He did not tell her that he had a child out of wedlock—nor, however, did he give her hopes of a possible marriage. Georg did not make it easy for Hilda. He often behaved aloofly and stubbornly, only to become kind and charming again, but he never offered Hilda a sense of unconditional security. He was not capable of that. Hilda practically had to fight for his affection and tenderness, and she only rarely succeeded; an invisible barrier always remained. Sometimes she had the feeling that Georg was standing in his own way. She tried to imagine what went on in his head, what thoughts preoccupied him, what emotions blocked him. Georg did not talk much about things like that. He was a practical person—not someone who communicated well with words.

For almost two years he worked in Meersburg, and then he and his colleagues were given notice that the company had to file for bankruptcy again. Georg quickly found another job in a small carpenter's workshop in the immediate vicinity, where he was tasked mainly with making doorframes and doors. But after five weeks, he was laid off there, too, because there were no more orders.

In May 1932, after unsuccessful attempts to find a new job, Georg gave up his room in Konstanz and moved to Meersburg, where he repaired furniture and made small items for various people in exchange for room and board. Later he recalled:

At that time, I worked for the widow Bechtle, who resides on the property of the master glazier Mauer. There I had to repair a secretary and build a table. At the moment I cannot remember other jobs I did for Frau Bechtle.

From Frau Bechtle, who was a good friend of the Doderer family, I received my meals at that time. For the overnight lodging I did not have to pay anything to D. After that I had to repair cabinets for the H. family, who were also good friends of the Doderer family—I no longer recall the apartment. I still occupied my apartment, that is, my room with D. at the time, but the H. family provided my meals. I remember that I also had to repair a cabinet for an Ottmar family during that same period. For the Doderer family, too, I had to fix an old cabinet.

In late July or early August 1932, I moved into accommodations in the home of Frau Sattler, whose bedroom I had to renovate.

I only gave up the room with D. because Frau Sattler had offered me lodging. I had my own small room there. The work for Frau Sattler lasted until about mid-August 1932.

These private carpentry jobs could not satisfy Georg in the long run. He also felt isolated in Meersburg, where he missed the evenings with the traditional costume society in Konstanz.

81

There, in a clear-cut setting, he had found cordiality, occasionally even recognition, which had meant a lot to him, perhaps even more than intense friendships. Only Hilda visited him now and then. Together they would walk along the lakeside. Sometimes they would get a table in one of the cafés. Both of them had sensed a long time ago that they had increasingly drifted apart since Georg's departure from Konstanz and had no future together. In any case, Georg had already long since made a significant decision—to return to Königsbronn.

A few days after he had begun lodging with Frau Bechtle, he had received a letter from his mother, in which she wrote that his father was drunk more and more often and was selling one field after another to pay his debts, which arose from the drinking and the neglected lumber trade. "Please, Georg," she wrote, "come home—we need you." The family expected his return to lead to an improvement; above all, Georg was to bring his father to his senses—not an easy task.

At that time, I took the train to my parents' house in Königsbronn. There I stayed in a room with my brother. My mother and my brother were very pleased with my return, while my father accepted it with indifference. I realized that my parents were in heavy debt due to my father's lumber trade, though I cannot say the exact amount. The debts were due in particular to the fact that my father bid too high for wood at auction and could only sell it again at a loss. From my uncle E. E. in Königsbronn, I learned that my father had always been under the influence of alcohol at wood auctions and that was the only reason he offered high prices. My father had been drinking beer and wine almost daily in Königsbronn and its environs, where he had business to do. I don't know the exact quantities. Neither my mother nor my brother had been able to exert an influence on him.

Thus he described, years later, his return to his parents' house. A return to the past? Almost. There was, however, one change. In the Reichstag elections on July 31, 1932, the National Socialists had achieved their breakthrough in Königsbronn. The Nazi Party received 38 percent of the votes. Among the people's cries of "Sieg Heil," abetted by the state and the economy, the path to catastrophe had begun—in Königsbronn, too.

CHAPTER NINE

Return to a "German Village"

January 30, 1933: Adolf Hitler is appointed the new chancel-lor of Germany by the aged President Hindenburg. His cabinet of the "national awakening" consists of nine ministers belong-ing to the German National Party or unaffiliated with a party as opposed to only three National Socialists—besides Hitler, there's Frick as minister of the interior and Göring as minister without portfolio. But the optical effect is illusory. The three National Socialist ministers have long held more power in their hands than the nine conservatives.

January 30 is their day, their victory. Ever since their pitiful putsch attempt ten years ago in the Munich Bürgerbräu Beer Hall, they have been waiting for this day of triumph.

On Wilhelmstrasse 77 in Berlin, formerly Bismarck's official residence, Hindenburg reads the oath of office with the shaky voice of old age, and has each member of the cabinet repeat it. Hitler is the first to swear the oath: *I will devote my strength to the welfare of the German people, preserve the constitution and the laws of the Reich, fulfill my duties conscientiously and conduct my affairs impar-tially and justly toward everyone.*

After the swearing-in, Hitler, with his two loyalists in tow, leaves the residence of the president, who sent off his new cabinet—the last of the Weimar Republic—with the words, "And now, gentlemen, forward with God."

Stepping out of the elevator in the Hotel Kaiserhof minutes later amid the cheers of his followers, Hitler cries, "Now we have made it!" They all shake his hand: Goebbels, Hess, Röhm—the line of well-wishers is endless. In the afternoon, the official announcement goes out into the Reich: *The President has appointed Adolf Hitler chancellor!*

Meanwhile, the party is already in the midst of organizing the evening celebration under Goebbels's leadership. The new Nazi minister of the interior, Frick, willingly lifts the restrictions in the government quarter. From seven o'clock in the evening until after midnight, 25,000 Hitler supporters, together with Stahlhelm units, march through the Brandenburg Gate in a torchlight parade.

When the celebratory procession reaches the brightly illuminated façade of the Reich Chancellery, the chorus of thousands of voices shouting "Heil" swells. In one of the windows, Adolf Hitler stands triumphant. In a dark suit, nervous and excited, he greets with a raised arm the masses marching past. Behind him are Göring, Frick, and other cabinet members. The cheers rise to a deafening roar. Not far from there, on the balcony of the Kaiserhof, SA chief Röhm, Gauleiter Goebbels, and all the prominent Nazi figures take in their "victory parade."

That night, after the cheering has fallen silent, after the military music and the sound of marching have faded, Hitler, surrounded by his closest confidants and "old fighters," remains in the Reich Chancellery until the early hours of the morning. He loses himself in endless monologues and speaks of having attained this goal only through divine providence. He recalls emotionally the scene of the morning's swearing-in ceremony with Hindenburg, mentions cheerfully the consternation of the "Reds," and finally asserts that this day marks the beginning of "the greatest Germanic racial revolution in world history."

* * *

In Königsbronn, the night after January 30 was a night like any other. For a long time, the lights had been turned out, the chairs had been put up in the Hecht tavern, and the last revelers had gone home. Only a yapping dog occasionally broke the silence.

Georg Elser rolled back and forth in bed, sleeping restlessly. After a while, he woke up completely, sat on the edge of the bed, rubbed his eyes, and ran his hands through his hair. How often had he sat like this in recent nights? There they were again, the snatches of dreams, the anxious thoughts, and the wishful fantasies. They made his head heavy, deprived him of sleep.

For six months now, he had been in Königsbronn helping his mother on the farm and occasionally assisting his father with the lumber trade. He had not found a job as a carpenter. Meanwhile, the household expenses were paid with the modest revenue from the farm work, for the lumber trade generated only deficits. His father reacted to criticism dismissively and aggressively. The whole family was oppressed by this situation. Georg—who had planned to exert his influence after his return to change the demoralizing circumstances in his parents' house—was the most deeply disappointed of all. Gradually, he had to admit to himself that he had no chance against his father's alcoholism, against his moods and angry outbursts. He felt powerless. It affected him profoundly to witness how his mother was demeaned by his father, how she toiled on the farm alongside her household duties in order to put any food on the table at all. He suffered from the fact that all this was no secret to the neighbors. He felt ashamed when he imagined how his father, under the influence of alcohol, drank away what little money they had. In this dismal situation, there were no signs of improvement.

At night, when he woke up, he felt distraught and longed for morning, but the new day was only a copy of the previous one. Was there any way out? Later he recalled this time.

My father's drinking kept increasing. As a result, the debts kept growing, and he frequently had to sell fields to meet his obligations. I had repeatedly tried to influence my father in a favorable way, but had no success. My father did not listen to anyone, including me. The household expenses were paid with the proceeds from the harvest.

My father always came home late. When he was drunk, he would make a scene and rail against my mother, my brother, and me without any cause. He always declared that it was our fault that things were going downhill.

Georg joined the Königsbronn zither club and, a few weeks later, the choir Concordia. *I was looking for diversion from the circumstances at home in music,* he later said about this decision during his interrogations.

When the orchestra needed an upright bass, he spontaneously took up the instrument. After a few weeks, he was able to play the upright bass at public performances. Georg was well liked in the groups, but he himself did not seek much contact with the other members. Just as he had relished participating in practice every Saturday evening at the Zum Kratzer inn as a member of the Upper Rhenish Traditional Costume Society during his time in Konstanz, he loved the rehearsals now, which took place every Friday in a side room of the Hecht tavern. Most of the time, the members' families, friends, and acquaintances were present at these rehearsals. It was always a large social gathering. When a concert or a dance was held in the Hösselsaal, things really livened up; on those occasions, Georg would forget his private problems for an evening and have a joyful time.

Apart from his participation in these groups, he had close contact only with his old childhood friend Eugen. He told him about his unsuccessful efforts to persuade his father to swear off alcohol, his arduous attempts to keep in check his father's increasing debts and save his parents' land from being put up for sale. He also spoke to his friend about his difficulties in finding a new job. Since his return, he had tried repeatedly to get a job as a carpenter, but to no avail.

Because he received no wages for his assistance in his parents' business, Georg had set up next to their house a small carpenter's workshop, which he called the "shed." There he made small repairs for neighbors and acquaintances, from which he earned some money.

Not until July 1934 did he find work again. The Königsbronn master carpenter Friedrich Grupp, a tall man with chiseled features and a friendly disposition, offered him a job as a journeyman for an hourly wage of 0.55 reichsmarks, and Georg immediately accepted. He finally had another opportunity to demonstrate his handicraft abilities and practice the occupation he loved.

Over the previous years—especially during his travels—he had acquired a great variety of skills and qualifications in his craft. He took each task as a challenge; the more difficult the work was, the more interesting he found it. He was most content to work alone and undisturbed. He didn't like it when his master looked over his shoulder, gave him well-meaning advice, or even nagged him. In the workshop, too, Georg was a loner and at times even an eccentric. Sometimes he overdid his desire to give everything 100 percent. Master carpenter Grupp later described his journeyman's work habits.

> *When he was done with his work, he would stand over it, staring thoughtfully for a long time. Then he would circle the worktable two or three times, viewing the piece from all sides. He knocked on it, shook it, checked everything, stepped back again to observe it from a distance, scrutinized it again thoroughly—and only then was the piece delivered. Then you could count on Georg to show up the next day at the people's home and say he would like to look at the piece again and make sure that everything was all right. He would then examine it again. He really had a downright fussy nature. He worked extremely meticulously.*

Georg saw himself as an "artistic carpenter" as opposed to an ordinary one. He never looked for a job merely for the sake of a secure existence, but rather in order to be *creatively active,* as he once put it. Perhaps this was a central motivation for his frequent changes of employment. What mattered to him was not only receiving fair, standard compensation, but also being able to work independently and without a master hovering over him. What was most important to him was the inner satisfaction he felt after completing a piece of furniture. Creative self-development was a priority; he based his identity on it. Master carpenter Grupp later recalled:

> *He was a good craftsman, thoroughly decent and honest. And to my delight, he worked overtime. When something had to be done, he did it. It was only necessary for my wife to put a piece of cake on the workbench*

for him, and he was content. He always built for himself alone. He was
a real loner. Once I considered producing a complete bedroom. At the
time, that was out of the ordinary for a small workshop.

Grupp had received the catalog of a furniture factory and called
his journeyman over to ask him whether they should make a
bedroom like that, too. "Let's do it," said Elser. "But I have to
redesign it. I'll make it better."

The next day, recounted the master carpenter, his journeyman brought polished drawings, which he had apparently made
the previous night. They had spoken about it for at most half an
hour, and then Elser set to work. In the days that followed, they
said scarcely a word to each other. Grupp gave no instructions at
all, and his journeyman didn't have any questions. After fourteen
days, the bedroom was finished; the work was so clean and precise
that his wife didn't want to sell it. But then an acquaintance from
the village absolutely had to have it and bought it. It was a magnif-
icent piece of work that Georg had carpentered, Grupp recalled.

When Elser quit after only four months, the master carpenter was, understandably, not exactly thrilled about it, but nothing he could say was of any use. Elser would not change his mind.
Might his quitting have had something to do with the fact that any
amount over twenty-four reichsmarks was taken out of his weekly
wages to pay alimony? Twice the youth welfare office had inquired
with the master carpenter regarding the alimony payments for
Elser's illegitimate son. At that point, Grupp suggested an internal solution with which they might be able to avoid the authorities'
access to Elser's weekly wages. But the journeyman declined. "No,
that's all right. My quitting had nothing to do with that. I have to
deal with our property at home before it's too late."

Like most Königsbronn residents, master carpenter Grupp knew
about the alcoholic escapades of Georg's father. Secretly, he even
respected his journeyman's decision to quit his job in order to help
save his family from financial ruin and a fall in social position—
a risky undertaking at a time when things did not look rosy
with jobs up in the eastern Swabian Alps. In the big cities, the
National Socialists had to some extent been able to convey the
impression that they were getting the mass unemployment under

control, but that was not the case here in the provinces, where increasing industrialization had caused serious distress for the traditionally medium-sized trades in the countryside. Small businesses, such as that of master carpenter Grupp, were not equipped for mass production. Many carpenters' workshops had to close, including in the eastern Swabian Alps.

As before, Georg helped his mother on the farm and tried as much as he could to restrain his father's erratic and irascible character, but his efforts were all in vain. The illusions of his mother—who after Georg's return had still believed that things would somehow be all right and that her husband's drinking would, at last, come to an end—increasingly dissipated. Her hope had turned out to be mere naïveté. Georg later described the fatal development.

At the end of 1935, the debts were so large that my father had to sell the property, which by my estimate was worth between 10,000 and 11,000 reichsmarks. He sold it for 6,500 reichsmarks to the cattle dealer M. in Königsbronn, who regularly drank with him in taverns. From the proceeds of the sale, my mother demanded and received 2,000 reichsmarks. The remainder my father used to pay his debts and to keep drinking. After the property was sold, the cattle dealer M. moved in. During the sale, it was agreed that a small room would remain available to my father.

The sale spelled the temporary end of the marriage. Shortly thereafter, Georg's mother moved in with her daughter Friederike, who had her own apartment with her husband Willy in nearby Schnaitheim. She took with her all the household items, fearing that her husband might sell them, too. Georg's father stayed behind; the new owner allowed him to continue living for a while under his former roof. Georg's brother Leonhard went into the labor service.

Georg rented a room in Elsa Heller's house. He had met her three years earlier on an excursion with the Königsbronn hiking club, which had since been compulsorily assigned to the *Kraft durch Freude* (Strength through Joy) movement, the state-controlled leisure program. On a hike into the Steinernes Meer near Bartholomä, a landscape typical of the eastern Schwabian Alps between Königsbronn and Aalen, the two of them had immediately felt a strong attraction to each other. Both sought a sense of security and emotional warmth. Their fates were extremely similar: Georg often felt lonely and oppressed by his father's alcoholism and the problems in his parents' house. Elsa lived with a carpenter to whom she was unhappily married, a coarse fellow who only sporadically pursued his work and was quick-tempered, unjust, and brutal toward her. He, too, drank a lot. Frequently, when he came home after a bout of drinking, he would beat her. Elsa told Georg how afraid she was for herself and her little daughter Iris. She trusted him. Georg was so different from her husband in every way. He didn't drink, didn't smoke, and was diligent and humble—never loud and unrestrained. In December 1935, Elsa had given birth to her second child, a boy, and more than a few Königsbronn residents who knew about the relationship between her and Georg suspected that he was the father. The entry in the birth register nonetheless listed Hermann Heller as the father.

In the spring of 1936, Georg moved into the Hellers' house as a tenant under the husband's suspicious glances. Hermann Heller had long suspected a love affair between his wife and the quiet, slight-looking tenant who had set up a workshop for himself in the basement of their house. From the beginning, living together under one roof turned out to be oppressive, even agonizing, for everyone—especially for Elsa. She, who now longed more and more for the end of her marriage and was thinking about divorce, reached the limit of what she could physically bear. She suffered from her husband's daily reproaches, his moods and outbursts, but also from the inaccessible proximity of her lover, who spent every evening puttering around in his workshop after he had finished his often ten-hour workday.

At that time, Elser was again working as a journeyman in the Königsbronn workshop of master carpenter Grupp—though not for long, as the transcript of his later interrogations shows.

In the spring of 1936, Grupp was commissioned to manufacture desks for the Wehrmacht, which had to be delivered at a specific time. For that reason, he had approached me to work for him. After finishing this delivery, I was working on apartment furnishings and putting in window frames in a building under renovation. In the autumn of 1936, I gave notice to Grupp, because, for one thing, the payment was too low for me and, for another, he always wanted to instruct me, even though he did not have the skills I had. I parted amicably from Grupp; I quit for the reasons mentioned in the firm belief that I would find work again soon.

As it would turn out, however, Elser was mistaken. At a time when handicraft abilities were in decreasing demand in favor of the efficient production of factory-made furniture, his prospects of finding a job in keeping with his ambitions diminished. Eventually, he also had to abandon his great dream of one day opening his own small workshop as a cabinetmaker. In addition, he faced growing debts due to neglected alimony payments for his illegitimate son. He thus increasingly had to suppress his secret wishes and longings.

After three months of renewed unemployment, Elser finally started a job at the end of December 1936 as an unskilled laborer in a fittings factory in Heidenheim.

I ended up there through the auspices of Wilhelm H., who was a foreman there. At the time, he was living in Itzelberg near Königsbronn, and I had met him in mid-December 1936 at the Rössl tavern in Königsbronn. I knew H. personally from his frequent stays in Königsbronn. In the course of our conversation, I told him about my current circumstances, and he suggested that I work as an unskilled laborer in the fittings factory in Heidenheim. I don't recall exactly whether I had already been looking for a job as a skilled carpenter at that time, but I think that I had found nothing of the sort, which prompted me to accept the job as an unskilled laborer. As far as I can remember, H. offered to inquire at his company, where he was a foreman, whether there were any openings. After a few days he informed me that the answer was yes, and I should introduce myself. I went to Heidenheim either by train or by bicycle, introduced myself, and was able to begin one or two days later as an unskilled laborer in the fettling shop, where H. worked as well. I was told that I would not do the dirty fettling work for long, but would soon be able to perform a more pleasant task. Indeed, I had to do this job for only about half a year, until the summer of 1937, when I entered the shipping department. There I was responsible for checking the completeness of the incoming material, etc.

He was not thrilled with his new work, but there were nonetheless reasons to stay.

In the fettling shop, I received 0.58 reichsmarks, later 0.62 reichsmarks per hour. It's true that as a skilled carpenter I would have gotten more elsewhere, but I was not interested in earning more, only in liking my work. If I had earned more, I wouldn't have reaped the benefits of it anyhow, because any amount over twenty-four reichsmarks was taken out of my weekly wages for the payment of alimony.

Elser was unhappy with his living situation as well. Since he had moved in with the Hellers, there had been a tense atmosphere. Elsa and he tried to arrange their love affair to the extent possible. But in December 1936, there was a quarrel. It began when Georg took on the task of making some kitchen furniture to settle the rent payments. Suddenly Elsa's husband forbade him from doing any more carpentry in the house. *I did not finish the kitchen cabinet after Mrs. H.'s husband called a halt to the work for reasons unknown to me*, he said in his interrogations regarding the confrontation.

In the spring of 1937, Elsa's husband terminated the rental agreement. Georg was almost happy about it. From the beginning, he had had a bad feeling about living under one roof with a couple whose marriage was falling apart while he was the wife's lover. Now this misbegotten situation had come to an end. But what options did he have left?

Once again, he returned to his parents, who had in the meantime reconciled and now lived in half of a duplex house on Sumpfwiesenstrasse in Königsbronn, which they had been able to buy with the proceeds from the sale of their former property. *In my parents' house, I stayed in an attic room. I also took with me my workshop, which I had set up provisionally in the H. house, and again set it up provisionally in a basement room of my parents' house.*

Eugen Rau, his childhood friend, who had in the meantime gotten married and started a family, lived next door. The two of them had remained friends, trusted each other, and often talked about circumstances and developments it had long since become unsafe to discuss publicly.

* * *

On June 22, 1933, the Nazis, newly in power, had issued a decree to combat the so-called "defeatist attitude," making the mere expression of dissatisfaction a punishable offense as a form of "Marxist agitation." In the years that followed, the National Socialists carried out all the necessary steps to become a Führer state: The party's organizational schema divided the country into thirty-two regions, which were further divided into districts, local branches, cells, and blocks. Hitler had once said, *What is the point of socializing factories and such things? We are socializing the people.* With his party organizations, he had after a short time achieved his goal of making an individual life in Germany almost impossible. First you were a *Pimpf* (a member of the Jungvolk, the ten- to fourteen-year-old subsection of the Hitler Youth), then you joined the Hitler Youth, and then you entered the SA or SS or went directly into the Nazi Party. As a driver, you were in the National Socialist Motor Corps; as a young girl, you were in the League of German Girls. No sports association, no hiking group, no amateur theater could escape the reach of Gleichschaltung.

Königsbronn was no exception. The traditional village fairs had long been supplanted by the Nazi holiday calendar. On January 30, swastika flags fluttered in the village streets, as the Reich Flag Law prescribed. With an abundance of rallies, commemorations, and parades, the local party branches ensured that the image of the Führer appeared virtually ubiquitous.

Nor could the National Socialists complain about a lack of popularity in the provinces. To be sure, it had not been necessary, as it had been in the cities after the Nazis came to power, to declare a temporary cap on new members due to the huge rush; effective May 1, 1933, the party's regional leadership had been instructed to accept new party members only into the Hitler Youth, the SA, and the SS. Though the rush in the eastern Swabian Alps had not been quite as intense, members flocked to the new national movement in droves there as well. As early as February 25, 1934, Hitler's deputy Rudolf Hess, on the radio from Königsplatz in Munich amid the roar of cannons, had administered an oath to almost a million party members: *Adolf Hitler is Germany, and Germany is Adolf Hitler. He who pledges an oath to Hitler pledges an oath to Germany.*

Along with their counterparts all over the Reich, party members in Königsbronn listened with awe to the mass pledge. Here, too, the local party branch had begun to co-opt the cultural life and all the clubs and societies into the new national movement. Eugen Rau's private dance group, the local hiking club, and the leftist political parties, whose share of the vote in this region had always been markedly above the national average before the National Socialists took power—these organizations ceased to exist.

Königsbronn, too, had become a "German village"—a village in exemplary conformity with the deceptive propaganda image of the new regime.

* * *

This change over the past several years had not escaped the notice of Georg Elser and Eugen Rau. When the local party members crowded around the *Volksempfänger* (people's radio receiver) in the Hecht tavern to listen raptly to the voices of Goebbels and Hitler and to propose toasts to the "national revolution" at the end of the speeches, Georg and Eugen would leave the room. Politics was not their thing—especially not the politics of the National Socialists.

Regarding Elser's political attitudes, Georg Vollmann, the local branch leader of the party until 1938, later testified that he *was neutral, was not a member of any party, and did not get involved in any debates. While I was local branch leader, I once observed Elser turning around and leaving during a parade. That was no big deal, but it struck me that he was no man of the Third Reich.*

While the local branches in the provinces were marching in street parades, a first wave of "purges" had already claimed numerous victims throughout the Reich. More than eighty people—including "old fighters," SA comrades, and troublesome opponents—were murdered on the "Night of the Long Knives," when the so-called Röhm Putsch was put down at the end of June 1934. This time, no one could speak of a "night of the miracle," as the propagandists had when Hitler gained power. Instead, the Nazi regime carried out a "night of terror," committing a series of political murders. Among the victims were former chancellor Kurt von Schleicher; his closest colleague

General von Bredow; the former Reichsorganisationsleiter of the Nazi Party Gregor Strasser; and Gustav von Kahr, whom Hitler had urged to join his putsch in Munich in 1923. Father Bernhard Stempfle, editor of the *Miesbacher Anzeiger*, who was credited in party circles with having helped the Führer compose *Mein Kampf*, was killed in cold blood, as were the closest colleagues of Vice-Chancellor von Papen.

On July 2, 1934, Hitler expelled the dead Röhm from the SA and the party. At the same time, a man named Heinrich Himmler stepped forward as chief of the SS. When President Paul von Hindenburg died that same year on August 2, Hitler's last hurdle on the path to absolute power had been removed. Now he appointed himself head of state—one people, one Reich, one Führer.

With the exception of the victims, not many Germans seemed interested in the fact that a year later an unknown ministry official named Hans Globke—who would become quite well known after the world war as Chancellor Konrad Adenauer's state secretary—wrote a commentary on the Nuremberg Laws that ushered in a previously unimaginable degradation and persecution of the Jewish population. It was more important to the German Volk that there were no longer 6 million unemployed, but only 2.5 million. The propaganda organizations of the Nazi regime disseminated their "success reports" into the most remote corners of the Reich, while the party faithful in the regions and villages cheered with their shouts of "Heil," hung swastika flags in their windows, and marched in step through the village streets—in Königsbronn, too. There were few who did not join in the Greater German jubilation.

Among them was Georg Elser, who not only lacked enthusiasm for the Third Reich, but also had never liked political debates and demonstrations.

My parents have always been completely apolitical. I remember that my father only voted when someone came to get him. I don't know whom he voted for. When I reached voting age, he definitely never influenced me in any way. I think my mother voted, but she never said anything about whom she voted for, he later testified during his interrogations in Berlin, in response to questioning about his political development.

His mother confirmed those statements: *In our family no one was really concerned with politics. My husband wasn't interested in it. You did your work and didn't worry about parties and politics.* If a political topic did come up, Georg uttered one or two sentences and then let the matter rest.

He had almost nothing to say about politics and was not at all interested in it. If I myself or other people grumbled in his presence about measures taken by the Nazi Party, he was always very consistent in his statements. He always said: You're either for them or against them, his girlfriend Elsa recalled. Once, before an election in Königsbronn, she had spoken to him about politics. She had asked him whether he was going to vote, and he had said no. She tried to persuade him to vote, because she was afraid that there might be talk in the small village, but that didn't matter to him. *What do I care what other people say,* he responded. Nonetheless, he had no objections to her voting. *You have to decide that for yourself,* he told her.

Where did it come from, his intuitive aversion to the Nazi regime? Where did this categorical rejection come from? He explained the reasons for it during his interrogation in Berlin.

> *In my view, circumstances after the national revolution worsened in various ways. For example, I noticed that wages got lower and deductions higher. Furthermore, the workers, in my view, have been under certain constraints since the national revolution. For example, the worker can no longer freely change his place of work as he pleases. Because of the Hitler Youth, he is no longer the master of his children. And he can no longer act so freely with respect to religion.*

Though Elser rarely took part in political discussions, he was regarded as leaning toward the left. On the one hand, that might have had to do with the fact that anyone who did not agree with the National Socialists was immediately branded a "communist" and declared an enemy of the people. On the other hand, he did feel most comfortable in like-minded circles, where he could presume kindred attitudes without first having long discussions about politics.

Among the Friends of Nature and the hiking club, which he had joined during his stay in Konstanz, he found an unspoken accord with his sense of what was going on around him, with the way he saw his everyday life and his problems. At that time, he also joined the Red Front Fighters League (Rotfrontkämpferbund, RFB), a militant group associated with the Communist Party. Their sign was a balled fist. Did this membership suit him and his behavior in general?

I was only a dues-paying member, for I never wore a uniform or occupied any official post. Only three times during my whole RFB membership did I attend political meetings—of the Communist Party, of course. I joined the RFB after frequent coaxing by a colleague named F., who was working, as I was, in the clock factory in Konstanz, he later stated.

In Konstanz and Königsbronn, his political attitudes were not the result of ideological thinking, but the expression of his observations of his immediate social surroundings—particularly his firsthand impression that National Socialist policies by no means improved the economic situation of the workers (as Nazi propaganda would have had people believe), but actually worsened them. This deeply aroused his sense of justice.

I was a member of the woodworkers' union, because this was the organization of workers in my profession and because you were supposed to be a member of this organization. . . .

Personally, I never got involved in politics. After reaching voting age, I always voted for the Communist Party, because I thought it was a worker's party and would definitely advocate for the workers, but I never became a member of the party, because I thought it was enough to give them my vote. . . .

As to whether I knew that the Communist Party had the intention and the goal of establishing in Germany a Soviet-style dictatorship or a dictatorship of the proletariat, I have to say that it is not impossible that I heard something like that at some point. But I definitely didn't think anything of it. All I thought was that you had to strengthen the Communists' mandate by giving them your vote so that the party could do more for the workers. I never heard anything about a violent overthrow.

I was never interested in the program of the Communist Party. So I cannot say how the economic situation would have changed in the event of a Communist victory. All that was discussed at the meetings was that there should be higher wages, better housing, and things like that.

The statement of those demands was enough to make me lean toward the Communists.

In the summer of 1937, Elser rode his bike every morning, weather permitting, to work in Heidenheim. On the way, he lost himself in his thoughts. What would his future be like, especially his relationship with Elsa, who had filed for divorce, left the house she shared with her husband, and moved to her parents' house in Jebenhausen? On the one hand, he felt secure with Elsa; he loved her almost maternal way of caring for him. Hadn't he always longed for this affection? His rapport with her parents was good, too. They accepted him—more than that, her father had even offered a few days ago to finance courses in interior architecture for him. "You're an intelligent fellow," he had said. "You can make something of yourself." Plus, Elsa's parents had held out the prospect of an apartment in their own house for the two of them. "We would just give notice to the tenants," her father said. Georg had declined both offers. He didn't want others to be kicked out for his sake; nor did he want Elsa's father to pay for his studies. No, he didn't want to have his future made for him, he told Elsa.

He understood that Elsa's parents were motivated by their desire to help their daughter and her two small children get back on their feet after a failed marriage. Georg seemed to them to be the right man for that. With him by her side, they thought, their daughter Elsa could once again find family happiness. Now, as the first Heidenheim houses were emerging from the morning mist, he thought about the fact that he had once promised to marry Elsa. She should get a divorce, he had told her, and then they could get married. But afterward, he had been overcome by doubts. Could he feed a family? Did he even have a chance of earning enough money in the foreseeable future despite his deductions for the alimony payments?

He had spoken to Elsa about that, and she had tried to reassure him. We'll manage, she had told him. Where there's a will, there's a way. But did he want to continue on this path? For all the love he felt for her, was Elsa the woman with whom he wanted to spend the rest of his life? What if their interests, their characters were too different? Their plans? His plans? What was going to happen with his work? He did not want to work as an unskilled laborer in the long run; though it paid well, it had nothing to do with the craft he had learned and was not what he envisioned doing. How would he escape the cramped circumstances in his parents' house, where they had now even demanded rent from him for an attic room—a demand he had refused on the grounds that he had worked for years without pay in his parents' business? How long would he continue to endure his mother's disapproving glances when Elsa visited him in his room?

Georg was anything but happy that morning. His life seemed to be at an impasse; his own life felt foreign to him. Was there a new prospect in sight? *The whole year of 1937 and a large part of 1938 passed without events or changes*, he said later in his interrogations. Everything repeated itself: work, the end of the workday, the weekends, the weekly rehearsals with the zither club. Georg experienced a sense of stagnation. His everyday life had become a rigid ritual.

* * *

More so than in previous years, Georg lived the life of a loner. He maintained contact only with Elsa and Eugen. The two of them were the only people whose closeness he not only accepted, but also sought. In taverns, where he often took his meals, he remained a perpetual outsider. There he sat, withdrawn and alone—observing, listening, ruminating. He did what scarcely anyone else did at that time: he measured the Nazi propaganda against social reality. And he made comparisons. During his interrogations in the Berlin Gestapo building, he testified:

> *When I was earning fifty reichsmarks per week on average in the clock factory in Konstanz in 1929, the deductions for taxes, health insurance, unemployment benefits, and disability insurance amounted to only about five reichsmarks. Today the deductions are already that high for weekly earnings of twenty-five reichsmarks. The hourly wage of a carpenter was one reichsmark in 1929; today an hourly wage of only sixty-eight pfennigs is paid. I can even remember an hourly wage of 1.05 reichsmarks being paid in 1929.*

From conversations with various workers, I know that in other occupations, too, the wages declined and the deductions increased after the national revolution. . . .

I made these observations and conclusions in the years leading up to 1938 as well as in the period that followed. Over that time, I realized that the workers are "angry" at the regime for these reasons. I came to these conclusions in general; individual people who said things in this vein I cannot recall. I made these observations in the places where I worked, in taverns, and on the train. I cannot give the names of any individual people, because I don't know them.

In all his testimony, he was careful not to cause trouble for any colleagues, acquaintances, or friends. But for all the dissatisfaction and "anger" he detected among his fellow workers, it did not escape his notice that there was a majority who rejoiced—in Königsbronn, too. The national enthusiasm—the noisy, wild excitement that had seized the people deep into the provinces—was unabated. But he was not overcome by it. He viewed the regime as dishonest, cynical, and unjust. Whenever the Führer's voice blared from the radio in the Hecht tavern, he left the room. The grandiose national spectacle provoked in him an intuitive aversion. Amid the myriad shouts of "Heil," he felt his doubts mounting to despair.

Was there a way out—private or political? His thoughts overwhelmed him. Deadly thoughts . . .

CHAPTER TEN

The Decision—The Plan

The train rolled slowly into the Munich station. The clock hand moved to seven in the evening as the steam locomotive came to a stop with a loud screech and hiss. The platform and the vast ticket hall were crowded and hectic. A strikingly large number of people were wearing party uniforms. Georg Elser, dressed in a dark wool coat and holding a small travel bag in his right hand, looked even less conspicuous than usual on that evening of November 8, 1938. His slight figure got lost in the uniformed masses. He hastily crossed the hall and then turned right into an adjoining building. Over its entrance was the sign ACCOMMO-DATIONS OFFICE. He got into the line of people waiting. After a while, he was able to enter.

> In this room were several counters. Some members of the public and the staff of the accommodations office were in party uniform, while others were in civilian clothing. I no longer recall whether I was asked for my name and hometown or whether I was asked if I had been a participant in the march in 1923. I believe that I was asked only in what area I would like to stay.
>
> I did not make a particular request in this regard. I was simply handed a piece of paper with the note "Albanistrasse, house number and landlord". . . Whether I had to pay anything for the accommodations, I don't remember. From the accommodations office I proceeded directly to Albanistrasse. Because I didn't know my way around Munich, I took the streetcar there.

I asked a streetcar conductor for directions to the apartment. On my arrival, I found out that there were no overnight accommodations available. The people attended to me and put me up one floor below with a family whose name I have since forgotten. As far as I recall, I had to sleep on the sofa. I registered my occupancy with the police. When the people asked me, I gave them my real name, Georg Elser, and my place of residence, Königsbronn. I told these people that I only wanted to see Munich.

But Elser had not come to Munich to visit famous tourist destinations such as the Bavaria statue, the Frauenkirche, and the Hofbräuhaus. He had boarded the train in Königsbronn that morning in the knowledge that the reason for his journey could cost him his life. He had traveled via Ulm to the Bavarian metropolis to make the initial preparations for his plan to eliminate the Nazi leadership. He had decided to kill Hitler—on his own. From the daily paper he had learned about the annual meeting of the "old fighters" at the Munich Bürgerbräu Beer Hall, and now he was in this city to observe the course of the event. *At the time, I wanted to determine the prospects for putting my decision into action,* he later testified.

Around eight o'clock in the evening, Elser left his accommodations on Albanistrasse to walk to the Bürgerbräu Beer Hall in the Haidhausen district. Following directions from the people he was staying with, he started out along the Isar and then crossed the street to head up Rosenheimer Strasse toward the Bürgerbräu Beer Hall. At the point where Hochstrasse turned off to the right, heavy police units blocked the road. On the sidewalk, an endless line had formed, made up of people who had not been admitted into the long-since packed hall. Now they were waiting to see one prominent party figure or another departing after the rally, perhaps even—if only for a few seconds—the Führer. Many of the people had appeared in party uniform. Elser stood in the middle of the crowd until half past ten, when the roadblock was lifted and the masses gradually dispersed. The noise of enthusiasm that had greeted the party leaders as they left the Bürgerbräu Beer Hall faded.

Elser now continued up Rosenheimer Strasse, straight toward the illuminated entrance of the Bürgerbräu Beer Hall. Inside, a small group of brownshirts was finishing the last round of beer. Stuffy, thick air hung over the chairs and benches. Just a short while ago, almost three thousand National Socialists had been listening to the Führer's speech, euphorically applauding his remarks and hateful tirades. At the end, the excited listeners burst into shouts of "Heil," their right arms extended in front of them in the "German salute."

Now the staff was busy clearing the beer mugs and glasses from the tables. As they did every year, the resourceful waiters sold the glass from which the Führer had drunk during his speech to the highest bidder among Hitler's numerous female admirers, who had paid homage to their beloved Führer by rapturously kissing the large swastika flag hanging down from a pillar behind the lectern.

Elser went from the main entrance through the coatroom, directly into the hall. He proceeded to the middle of the hall and gathered his first impressions, as he described later during his interrogations:

> *I observed the hall, determined the location of the lectern, and viewed the decorations. I did not go onto the gallery itself. While I was there, I did not consider the best way to carry out an assassination in the hall.*
>
> *After I had examined the layout of the hall, I went from there through the coatroom into the so-called Bräustüberl of the Bürgerbräu Beer Hall, where I sat down at the first table for dinner.*

Around midnight he left the Bräustüberl and headed to his accommodations. There he proceeded to the room assigned to him, lay down on the sofa, and tried to fall asleep.

It occurred to him that the hall was not guarded in any way, that there was no security inspection at all, and that it was apparently possible to enter at any time. Could the organizers be that careless? Did they feel that safe?

At nine o'clock in the morning on November 9, he said goodbye to his hosts after breakfast. For the accommodations, he voluntarily paid them one reichsmark. He then walked the now-familiar route to the Bürgerbräu Beer Hall to see the start of the parade commemorating the "fallen of the movement." Three years earlier, in the course of a pompous ceremony that had since become a ritual, Hitler had for the first time honored those who had lost their lives in the march to the Feldherrnhalle on November 9, 1923. The architect Ludwig Troost had been commissioned to design a worthy memorial for the sixteen sarcophagi of the "martyrs." Since then, the National Socialist commemorative procession, with the Führer at the head, had made an annual pilgrimage from the Bürgerbräu Beer Hall to Königsplatz, where two immense, classicistic temples had been erected as National Socialist places of worship.

On this November 9, too, loudspeakers repeatedly broadcast the Horst Wessel Song along the route of the march, while thousands of National Socialists with countless flags and standards proceeded silently through the rows of onlookers. Elser was at once impressed and repelled. On the one hand, he was experiencing firsthand the dramaturgy of a Nazi mass spectacle. The uniformed silent march seemed to him like an endless funeral procession—a march to ruin. More clearly than ever, he felt his opposition, his resistance. Thoughts were going through his head that had long provided fertile ground for his assassination plans:

The dissatisfaction I had observed among the workers since 1933 and the war I had assumed to be inevitable since the fall of 1938 constantly preoccupied my thoughts. I no longer recall whether this was before or after the September crisis of 1938. I considered on my own how the circumstances of the workers could be improved and a war avoided. No one urged me to do so or influenced me in that direction; nor had I ever heard conversations along those lines. Not even from the Moscow radio station had I heard that the German regime should be overthrown. My considerations led to the conclusion that the circumstances in Germany could be changed only through an elimination of the current leadership. What I understood by leadership were the men at the very top—that is, Hitler, Göring, and Goebbels. As a result of my thinking, I became convinced that after the elimination of those three men, other men would take office who would not make unbearable demands on other countries, who would not attempt to appropriate foreign territory, and who would ensure an improvement in the social circumstances of the workers. Neither then nor later did I think of particular people who would take over the government. At the time, I did not want to eliminate National Socialism. I was convinced that National Socialism had the power in its hands and that it would not give it up. I was merely of the opinion that the elimi-nation of those three men would bring about the setting of more moder-ate political goals. I can say with certainty that I was not thinking at all of another party or organization that would have taken the reins in Germany after the elimination of the leadership. I did not speak to any-one about that point either. The idea of eliminating the leadership would give me no peace at that time, and in the autumn of 1938—this was before November 1938—I had made the decision based on my repeated considerations to carry out the elimination of the leadership myself.

In recent weeks, he had thought constantly about the politi-cal situation and spoken with Eugen about it. Would there be a war? In the wake of the Munich Agreement, Georg feared the possibility.

"Eugen," he had said on one of their walks together, "the regime will not be content with the Sudetenland. They've set their sights on other countries, too." Eugen nodded thoughtfully.

Another time they talked about the situation of the workers. "Things are worse for the workers now than they were several years ago," Georg complained. "These days, the deductions are higher and the wages lower."

"Yes, but what are you going to do?" Eugen replied with a shrug. "The workers vote for the Nazis. Everyone grumbles, but no one ever says his opinion out loud."

Georg nodded in agreement. He had been repeatedly con-fronted with these experiences. As an unskilled laborer in the Heidenheim fittings factory, he had seen his professional ideals steadily thwarted.

The conversations between the two men largely revolved around their everyday lives. As Georg's handicraft skills had fallen out of demand, he had been deprived of his only means of self-fulfillment. His perceptions and experiences at his job had first made him dispirited and later combative. Though he preferred not to talk about political topics, he always openly expressed his opinion, even when doing so was to his detri-ment, and he loathed nothing so much as quiet opportunism. In recent weeks, he had felt more and more clearly that he had to do something—to take action, resist.

After his return from Munich he came to the firm decision to put his assassination plans into action. The preparations could begin.

In the weeks that followed, I had gradually worked out in my head that it would be best to plant explosives in the column behind the speaker's podium and to detonate them with some sort of device at the right time. I did not yet have a clear conception of this detonation apparatus. I chose the column because the flying fragments in an explosion would strike the people at and around the lectern. I also thought that the ceiling might collapse. It is true that I did not know which people would be sitting around the lectern at the event, but I knew that Hitler would be speaking and assumed that the leadership would be sitting nearby. Up to that point, I had neither theoretical nor practical experience with the construction of any device with which explosives could be detonated at a particular time.

Thus he later described his initial considerations at his interrogations. He also explained how his job in the fittings factory served his purposes.

When I began working at the fittings factory in Heidenheim, there was already a so-called "special department" in which powder grains were pressed and shell detonators were produced. . . .

For this special department, samples and designs of detonators and detonator parts arrived, which I received for the company and which were passed on to the individual foremen in the special department after the delivery was inspected. In the shipping department, I was responsible for recording the arrival and the integrity of the deliveries.

In the powder press department, I had to deliver the received boxes and containers of powder to a worker. The name of this worker I have forgotten. There was no foreman there. From there I also had to take the empty boxes and containers back to the shipping department. I brought them to a room on the ground floor, where I gave them to a worker. The two assistants who had been assigned to me also helped with the delivery of the received orders of material. I was not friendly or more closely acquainted with the foremen or any worker employed in the special department. I knew those people only by sight. No one in the special department showed me how detonators are assembled and constructed. Nor did I ever watch

106

how such detonators were constructed. This was prohibited by the factory management. In the special department, I was only to deliver the received material and then leave immediately. . . .

Though I was not allowed to watch how detonators were assembled, I saw various component parts that passed through my hands, such as the pins for the detonation, and also often held in my hands drawings on which the exact measurements for the control gauges were indicated.

Without anyone noticing, Elser managed to steal two hundred packets of powder and hide them in his attic room. He later said:

As long as I was living at home, I kept the increasing supply of powder in my closet. I had wrapped the powder in paper, placed it at the bottom of the closet, and covered it with linens. No one in my family discovered the powder. I always locked my room.

There were reasons for his mistrust, as there had been disharmony in the house for months. It had all begun with the marriage of his brother Leonhard, who later recalled the cause of the conflict:

In 1938 I got married, and I had a quarrel with Georg at the time because I told him he had to leave the house. According to the entry for the house in the title register, a third belonged to me, a third to my father, and a third to my mother. Georg had no share in the house, and the dispute revolved around financial matters, because I wanted Georg to pay us rent, which he never did.

Their mother suffered most from the feud. She tried several times to propose a compromise, but Georg refused. After all he had done for his family over the previous years, he felt slighted and wronged. *That's when Georg stopped talking to us,* his mother later recalled.

Georg ultimately left his parents' house on hostile terms. The break was final. The family would not see each other again until the Gestapo interrogations in Berlin.

* * *

On April 4, 1939, at a counter in the Königsbronn train station, Georg bought a ticket to Ulm. There he boarded the express train to Munich. No one took particular notice of this journey. In March, he had quit his job in the Heidenheim fittings factory.

> *The reason I quit was a quarrel I had with the foreman of the apprentice department, who had repeatedly made rude remarks to me that I did not put up with because I was not subordinate to him. I was to open a package urgently that had arrived for him in the shipping department, which I did not consider necessary. It was not the case that I left the company only because I was afraid I would not be able to steal enough explosives. The factory manager did not accept my resignation. At that time, he became ill, and I turned to his deputy, who gave me my papers several days later after a number of appointments.*

There was no reason for him to mention his journey at home; he had decided that he would move out of his parents' house for good as soon as he was back from Munich. He did not even speak with Eugen about his plans and preparations. And with Elsa?

In the previous weeks, he had kept his contact with her to a minimum. Was it the lack of time? Had he lost interest in her? Or was he once again aware of the absence of prospects for their relationship? Was he distancing himself in order to avoid drawing Elsa into things she wouldn't understand? But who would understand?

A few days ago, he had begun to make his first sketches of an explosive device in his attic room. *Once I had worked out the rough design of the apparatus in my head,* he later stated, *I realized that it was necessary to have the exact measurements of the column in which I wanted to plant the apparatus.* So he had to go to Munich again. There he rented a room at an inn near Rosenheimer Platz under his real name.

No one took particular notice of the quiet guest. In the morning, he had his breakfast alone in a corner of the dining room. After that, he left and did not return until late in the evening. The innkeepers scarcely paid attention to him—and why should they? As long as a guest paid for his room and did not create any disturbance, he was welcome and you didn't ask about his comings and goings. The somewhat shy-seeming guest had paid in advance the overnight cost of two reichsmarks for eight days, and thus the taciturn man was among the innkeepers' favorite customers.

Elser had a lot to do. On the second day after his arrival in Munich, he went to the Bürgerbräu Beer Hall once again to make the necessary sketches. This time, too, the doors to the hall were open.

I no longer needed to consider where I would place my explosive device. I was already certain that it would be above the base of the gallery, so I proceeded immediately to the gallery. As far as I can remember, I went the shortest way, by the stairs to the left of the entrance. On the gallery, I then took the measurements of the column in question with a folding meter stick I'd brought with me and entered the dimensions in my notebook— that is, I made a small sketch in my notebook and marked the measurements on the sketch. I don't think that there was anyone else in the hall at that time—at least I can't remember seeing anyone. I left the hall again through the main exit. I might have spent about five minutes there in all.

After leaving the hall, he went into the Bräustüberl, which was to the left of the main entrance, and ordered a cup of coffee. Shortly thereafter, the busboy sat down at Elser's table to have a meal. The two of them struck up a conversation. The busboy told him that he had to join the military soon, which he was in no hurry to do, because he would certainly lose his job. Elser nodded thoughtfully. It occurred to him that it would be advantageous for the preparation of the attack if he could get the job opening up. "Can I become an busboy?" he asked, to his young tablemate's surprise. The busboy promised to ask the manager about it.

On the way back to his accommodations, Elser thought about what a stroke of luck it would be to get the job, for he would be able to save a lot of money. True, he had saved almost four hundred reichsmarks from his earnings at the Heidenheim fittings factory and from the sale of wood, some tools, and his upright bass, but he would have to budget well. With the busboy job, he could save the overnight costs in Munich and earn some additional money.

Elser began visiting the Bräustüberl daily. He would have his meal there and then check whether the doors to the hall were open and whether there were people inside. If he saw the bus-

109

boy, he would remind him about his promise to talk to the manager. When the busboy still had no information for him on the fifth day, Elser decided to ask the manager himself, as he testified in his interrogations.

> *He was very surprised to hear that his busboy was required to report for military service, and apparently, after his conversation with me, he scolded the busboy for keeping it from him. The busboy told me that afterward and reproached me for asking the manager without having warned him. Later, when I was sitting in the Bürgerbräu Beer Hall, the manager came to my table and told me that the job prospect would probably come to nothing, because he was hoping that his busboy's military service would be deferred. After that, I spoke to the busboy a few more times about the matter, treated him several times to a glass of beer, and ultimately promised him twenty reichsmarks in writing, later raising it to fifty, if he would get me the job in the event that he had to report for military duty after all.*

The young busboy was puzzled. "Why is the job so important to you?" he asked at their last meeting. Elser told him that it had always been his dream to move to Munich. The busboy was content with that answer.

*   *   *

On April 12, Elser rode third class on the train back to Königsbronn. He had gotten what he had needed: usable sketches of the column with the exact measurements, as well as some photographs of the inside of the hall. Shortly after his arrival in Heidenheim, he would bring the film to a photographer with whom he was acquainted.

In May 1939, Elser moved to Schnaitheim, where he lodged with the Sauler family as a tenant. He had met their daughter, Maria, at his job in Heidenheim. They developed a warm friendship that was soon in secret competition with his relationship with Elsa. Now divorced from her husband, Elsa was living with her two children at her parents' home in Jebenhausen.

With the Saulers, Georg felt at ease. They accepted his withdrawn nature, but they nonetheless always invited him to participate in their domestic life. Some evenings, though rarely, Georg gladly accepted the invitation to dinner. They would all sit together in the kitchen playing cards, chatting, or listening to the radio—even the so-called enemy stations.

The radio was there in the kitchen. On that radio, we—that is, whoever was in the kitchen at that moment—often listened to the Strasbourg station, as well as a Swiss station. In the evening, when the family was in bed, I would sometimes turn on the Moscow station and listen to German broadcasts by myself. The name "Moscow" was not marked on the radio. I did not listen to other stations there with the exception of German radio stations and perhaps once or twice an English station. I'm not familiar with the Freedom Station 29.8 or other stations of that sort. In the family circle, there would be discussions of the content of the broadcasts. I can no longer recall the details of those conversations, but I remember that we dismissed particular news items that were obviously false and talked about whether others might be accurate.

The Saulers liked their tenant. He was pleasant to talk to and had their trust. He had set up a small workshop for himself in the basement of their house. In the evening, he would retreat there to work. When they asked him at one point what he was "puttering around" with down there, he answered mysteriously, "I'm working on an invention, and it has to be kept absolutely secret until it is patented." The family marveled in disbelief. Georg, an inventor? He was capable of anything . . .

During that time, Elser lived more reclusively than ever. He subordinated his whole life to the intensive attack preparations. He was completely preoccupied with his plan—the bomb.

Four weeks before he had moved to Schnaitheim, he had applied for a job in a Königsbronn quarry, because he knew that they worked with explosives there.

The main reason I applied for work there was that I could obtain powder for the planned attack there, he confessed in his interrogations. He got a job as an unskilled laborer with an hourly wage of 0.70 reichsmarks.

In April 1939, I hired Elser after receiving his application. Elser was unemployed at the time, and I urgently needed people in my quarry.

111

Elser was unusually interested in the blasting technology. During a conversation with him, I learned that he hoped to get a job in his profession in the foreseeable future in Munich, the owner of the quarry recalled years later.

Elser did not directly perform blasting work, but he often had the opportunity to observe the preparations for it. And, far more importantly, he saw that the explosives, secured completely inadequately with only a door lock, were kept in a small concrete storehouse.

In my first weeks, I already began to unlawfully appropriate explosives. This happened for the first time when blasting operations were done near my work area. It was often the case that more explosives were taken from the small concrete storehouse than were required for the blasting. How much explosive material was needed for the blasting operations could always be determined only on-site. The excess explosives were placed at some distance from the areas to be blasted. Often it was five or eight or two explosive cartridges that were left there unattended. When I observed this, I went directly there and always appropriated one cartridge, which I put in my pocket. I always made sure beforehand that no one was watching me. I did this about eight times, always during working hours. This theft was apparently never noticed . . .

In the period that followed, Elser broke into the explosives storehouse several times at night and stole larger amounts of explosives and blasting caps, more than he would need for the attack. He opened the lock of the small concrete house with old keys from his parents' property in Königsbronn, which he had filed for this purpose.

In response to questioning during his later Gestapo interrogations, he described in detail his nightly break-ins.

After I had opened the door to the small storehouse, I went inside. I turned on the flashlight I'd brought with me and saw that there were two wooden boxes in the house, about eighty centimeters long and twenty-five to thirty centimeters wide and roughly thirty-five centimeters high. Both boxes were open and still half filled with explosive cartridges. In one of the boxes, "Donarit" was printed on the cartridges, and there was also a number printed on them, which I do not remember—probably the number one. In the other box, "Gelantine" was printed on the cartridges, though I can't say this with certainty. The cartridges were packed in cartons with about twenty to twenty-five in each one, and these were placed in the boxes.

On the day I was in the small storehouse for the first time, I took such a packet of about twenty cartridges. I don't remember whether they were Donarit or Gelantine cartridges. I then left the storehouse, locked the door with the same key, and headed home with the cartridges.

Elser hid the stolen explosives in a suitcase, which he kept in his room next to his bed. He always locked the suitcase and carried the key with him. It was a special suitcase, which looked inconspicuous from outside but contained two secret compartments and a double bottom. When Georg had been working on putting in the secret compartments one evening in his small workshop, Maria had surprised him.

"Why are you fiddling with that suitcase?" she had asked him in bewilderment.

Startled and irritated at first, he had hastened to give a plausible explanation: "I keep drawings for my invention in it."

Maria was content with the answer; perhaps it sounded credible because he had already mentioned his "invention" to the family from time to time.

The nightly thefts in the explosives storehouse remained undiscovered, because in the quarry, no account was kept of the purchase or the use of the explosive materials. As a result, no one knew the actual inventories—a fact that would earn the quarry owner more than a year in prison after the attack for violation of the security requirements for storage of explosives.

Perhaps that was the reason that during his interrogations he spawned a conspiracy theory portraying Georg Elser as a member of a plot. The quarry owner testified that a man named Karl Kuch, who had left Königsbronn and had become wealthy in Switzerland, was a shadowy spy with all sorts of connections. In his view, it was Kuch who incited Elser to carry out the attack in Munich.

Georg Elser was very well acquainted with Karl Kuch, who was Swiss and came once or twice a year to Königsbronn on vacation. It has been proven that the Swiss man was a spy. He also illegally transferred money to Switzerland for local businesspeople. Under the guise of making ship- ping crates for Kuch, Elser had very close ties with him.

Kuch was very well acquainted with my first wife. He was in Königsbronn for an extended period of time from May to June 1939. He once showed up at my apartment, put a leather pouch—which looked like a salesman's bag—on the table in front of me, and said, "You're a stupid fellow. With your whole quarry you earn far less than what I earn. Look at this—this is what I earn!" He showed me a pouch full of jewels of all sorts: rings, brooches, etc.

Then I told him that I did not want to earn my money the way he earned his, and Kuch replied, "I know, you're a National Socialist and have no interest in political events, but there are other people, too. We have an interest in something happening in Germany. Hitler's dictatorship can- not be maintained. Hitler will start another war this autumn. But it will bring him no great pleasure, because we will deal with Hitler this year!"

Kuch then remained in Königsbronn for a while longer, and on the eve of Pentecost, he organized a farewell party. He invited me, too, but I couldn't come because I had another business-related engagement. I then learned that this party at the Hirsch went on for a rather long time and was followed by an excursion to the train station tavern in Aalen. They had coffee there, and the waiter was said to have approached Kuch and shown him a telegram. Kuch then left the train station tavern in a hurry and headed back to Königsbronn with his wife. Between Oberkochen and Königsbronn, he drove into a tree and was dead.

Strangely enough, my chauffeur happened to witness this accident. He immediately rushed to the crashed car and pulled Frau and Herr Kuch out of it. At that point, Kuch asked him: "Is the Gestapo already here?"

The quarry owner sought to suggest with his testimony that he suspected ominous string-pullers behind the car crash—perhaps even a conspiracy that ultimately involved the Gestapo itself.

For him it was clear that Kuch had made connections in Switzerland with Hitler's opponents, who had nothing against National Socialism but a great deal against the Führer's war plans. Elser—the man who worked for him in the quarry and whose theft of explosives sent him to prison—was only the lackey. He carried out the orders . . .

Georg's brother Leonhard later expressed his doubts about the accuracy of the claim that Elser had been in contact with Kuch and that the two of them had nurtured attack plans together.

I knew Herr Kuch from Königsbronn by sight. He was born in Königsbronn but lived in Switzerland. Kuch often came to Königsbronn for visits, and I remember that Kuch stayed here in 1939 for some time. I don't know whether my brother was friendly with this Kuch, or whether he had any connection to him. I can say with certainty that Kuch never came to our house to see Georg, and Georg never mentioned being acquainted with Kuch or having any dealings with him—nor did I hear anything later, after the attack and after the collapse of the regime in 1945, about this Kuch having incited my brother to commit the attack.

Would Georg Elser, who spoke to no one about his attack plans, not even Elsa or Eugen, have discussed them with Kuch, of all people—a man he barely knew?

The conspiracy theory was clearly a product of the quarry owner's imagination. In his resentment about his prison sentence in Stuttgart, he gave free rein to his suspicions and confused speculations during his interrogations, constructing his own theories.

Elser had worked for him for only three weeks. On May 16, 1939, he had to seek medical attention because a large stone had fallen on his foot; he was diagnosed with a fracture. With a cast that reached from his foot to a few inches above his ankle, Elser spent the days after the accident lying on the sofa in the Saulers' kitchen. His disability gave him the opportunity to participate in their family life more than in the previous weeks—to eat with them and talk with them about how the future of National Socialist Germany might look and whether it was only a matter of time before a war broke out. He also now found enough time to pursue the technical questions that had to be solved for the production of the explosive device.

During the job in the quarry and even before then, my preparations for the attack had progressed in other ways. After I had obtained the measurements of the column on my Easter journey to Munich, I could at first figure out the construction of my device only on paper. On certain days, I sat for hours over sketches, which I always made myself, and thought about the possibility of an explosive effect—that is, how the device might look.

I already knew, of course, that you could blast with powder. In the quarry, I had watched this closely, and I had also observed that you had to plant the explosives as deeply as possible. In addition, I had seen that you need blasting caps to detonate the explosives. Since I could not use a fuse for my attack, as I could not stand nearby to light it, I had to find another way to set off the blasting caps. Though I had never seen the inside of a rifle, I could imagine that the firing of a rifle caused a spring to release and strike the bottom of the cartridge.

So my next thought was to detonate the blasting caps with the help of rifle ammunition. I rode S.'s bike (I had sold my own a long time ago.) to a shop in Heidenheim where bikes were repaired and sold, and where sewing machines, rifles, bike parts, and ammunition were sold. I don't know the name of the owner of this shop and cannot give the exact address, but I can describe where the shop is located. It is on a side street off Adolf-Hitler-Strasse, very close to the corner house of master lathe operator P. In this shop, I simply asked for rifle ammunition. The man who helped me, probably the owner (about forty-five years old, short, stout), asked me what caliber I needed. I replied by asking what he had. He mentioned some calibers from six to nine millimeters. Because the largest seemed best to me, I had him give me a full metal box of twenty-five or fifty nine-millimeter cartridges. I don't remember what price I paid. The salesman did not ask me for a hunting license or a weapon license; nor did he ask for what purpose I wanted the ammunition. The cartridges he gave me had a roughly one-centimeter long case, on which there was a lead bullet (completely round). The purchase of the ammunition took place in the month of June or July. I cannot provide a more exact date.

On July 22, 1939, the doctor declared Elser fit for work again, but he had long since decided not to return to the quarry. *From that point on, I lived only for the preparation of my attack*, he later testified.

To test whether the rifle cartridges he had purchased could set off a blasting cap, he had built a model, which he brought, hidden in an old leather bag on his bicycle rack, to his parents' orchard.

It was a hot July morning when people in Königsbronn heard several blasts. They assumed that the sounds were coming from the quarry.

Elser was satisfied with his attempts. Later, he said:

After the explosion, I determined that the one small wooden block in which I had packed the cartridge case and blasting cap had been torn apart. That proved to me that a blasting cap could be set off without a fuse. Only after the experiment had succeeded three or four times in a row was I content. A single explosion of the blasting cap would not have been sufficient proof for me that it could be set off by means of a cartridge.

That evening, he retreated to his room in Schnaitheim. Countless sketches lay on the table; next to them was the model he had made, a strange-looking construction. At first glance, it resembled an amateurish monstrosity, but there was actually an elaborate system behind it.

Two small wooden blocks are mounted firmly on a board. Holes are drilled horizontally through both blocks in the same direction. A cylindrical wooden rod with a coil spring on it is stuck into these holes. On one side, the coil spring is touching a fixed wooden block. On the other side, it lies against a third small, wooden block, which is inserted loosely in a hole over the wooden rod and can be moved between the two fixed wooden blocks. With this third wooden block, which is equipped with a nail on one side, the spring can be tightened. Opposite this nail is another, smaller hole in one of the fixed blocks, into which the cartridge case of the rifle ammunition with a blasting cap stuck into it can be inserted.

With those words, a Gestapo officer later described the model, when Elser had been instructed to sketch his construction once again before the eyes of the interrogators.

On that July evening, Elser tried repeatedly to find practical solutions to his problems on paper. The most difficult question was how to set off the device at a precisely predetermined time. He made sketch after sketch, constantly producing new variations, more precise designs, and more refined details. Deep into the night he sat at his table, kept awake by the ambition to find a feasible solution.

It was clear to me from the beginning that I would use a clock mechanism for it. I always had some parts at home for table clocks with a gong. For years, I had gotten these from the B. Ri. company in Villingen/Schwarzwald. In my free time, I often built, stained, tarnished, or polished clock cases in all sorts of forms, installed the clock mechanisms, and then sold the finished table clocks to acquaintances or gave them away as gifts. I remember that I got clockwork machinery for this purpose from another company as well, but I don't recall its name at the moment. I took with me perhaps about four such clock mechanisms when I left the R. company in Meersburg in the spring of 1932. When R. fell behind on his wage payments, I asked him for some material instead of cash, and he gave me four or five clock mechanisms. I also received a half-finished grandfather clock case, as well as some other tools that do not, however, have any connection to my later deed. At the time, I was entitled to wages from the R. Company in the amount of 176 reichsmarks. Outside the bankruptcy proceedings, R. gave me these things as a settlement.

The way I had originally imagined I would transfer the clock mechanism to my detonation apparatus differed from the way I ultimately did so. Originally—that is, before I went to Munich to carry out the deed—I had intended to link the mechanism of the clock to the detonation device by means of a car direction indicator and a battery. For that reason, I brought with me to Munich a battery and three car direction indicators, only one of which I would have needed.

Shortly before his planned departure for Munich, Elser was unexpectedly laid up for four days with a case of stomach flu. The Saulers took good care of him—especially Maria, who was sad when he told her that he was planning to go to Munich. He had been offered a job as a carpenter there, he said, and he couldn't say no, especially as he had always wanted to move to Munich. Maria, too, dreamed of one day leaving Schnaitheim. To go out into a big city, a "world city" like Munich—that would be something. Ultimately, however, she lacked the courage for it. She had grown up here in the Swabian Alps; she felt rooted and at home here. She admired Georg for his decisiveness. He was moving to Munich, expanding his horizons.

For Elser, other thoughts were bound up with Munich. Would the attack succeed? Would it be possible to plant the bomb undetected in one of the columns?

He was nervous. In the previous days, he had already burned all unnecessary sketches and erased all possible traces in his small workshop. He thought of Munich, of the Bürgerbräu Beer Hall, of November 8 . . .

Perhaps those thoughts had upset his stomach? Just as he had begun to pack in boxes everything he thought he needed for the preparation and execution of the deed, he had been overcome by dizziness and his vision had blurred. Shortly thereafter, he had come down with a fever. Not until a day before his departure from Schnaitheim had he finally found time to stow the material in the secret compartments and the double bottom of his wooden suitcase. There were another two boxes containing his tools, which the Saulers would send to him in Munich. Had he forgotten anything? The evening before his departure, he went once again through the list:

- 250 packets of gunpowder
- 150 explosive cartridges
- More than a hundred blasting caps
- Five clock mechanisms
- One battery
- Several hammers, chisels, pliers, drills, and various wood-
  working tools

On August 5, the time had finally come. Georg Elser carefully lifted his wooden suitcase onto the luggage rack and placed another suitcase on top of it, containing clothes, linens, and personal items.

He opened the train window and leaned out. "Take care. I'll write to you . . . and again—many thanks for everything."

The train slowly began to move. Maria stood on the platform with tears in her eyes. As long as he could see her, Georg waved from the window. She returned his silent farewells with subdued gestures. Then he closed the window. He gazed out at the passing landscape. Was it a good-bye forever? He knew there was no going back.

119

CHAPTER ELEVEN

The Nights in the Hall

It was dark in the Bürgerbräu Beer Hall, with the emergency lighting only faintly illuminating the outlines of objects. The place smelled of stale beer, cigarette smoke, and dust—a pungent mixture. Erni Magerl left the Bräustüberl kitchen, walking down the corridor and through one of the wide, wooden doors that led under the gallery into the hall. The glow of her flashlight was the signal for the cats, which scurried over from all directions and crowded around the plate, greedily devouring the kitchen scraps. She had been working as a cigarette woman in the Bürgerbräu for more than ten years, and from the beginning, she had fed the cats every evening shortly before she got off work. Over the years, she had developed a personal relationship with the animals. She had given several of them names and ensured that some of their newborn kittens ended up in good hands, so that the number of cats remained in appropriate proportion to the size of the hall.

It was about half past ten when Erni was startled by an unfamiliar sound. Was it coming from the gallery? Was someone there? For a moment, she stood still and listened in the quiet hall.

Maybe it was a drunk? With rapid steps, she went back to the door to call for the janitor. "Coming," Xaver Hartgruber said, reassuring his colleague as he hurried over. A somewhat stout, round man of almost fifty years, he had long been—as the waiters liked to quip—part of the "inventory." Hartgruber regarded it as a "professional honor" to be the janitor of the

Bürgerbräu Beer Hall. A party member himself, he was proud that the "old fighters" had their annual meetings in "his" hall. Unprompted, he glowingly told everyone about the "great moment" when the Führer had personally shaken his hand once after the event. He had a photo of it in his living room at home. Hartgruber was a proper, nationally minded, "patriotic" janitor.

At around eleven o'clock, he entered the gallery. The glow of his flashlight illuminated the rear wall, but he found nothing suspicious and didn't hear a sound. Shaking his head, Hartgruber left the gallery by the back staircase. As he did every evening at that time, he locked the doors to the hall.

Georg Elser heaved a sigh of relief. His heart was pounding. He slowly felt his way out of the dark room in which he had hidden for more than half an hour—a storeroom, full of empty cardboard boxes, the entrance to which was covered by nothing but a folding screen facing the gallery. Once again he stood still, straining to listen in order to make sure that there really wasn't anyone in the hall anymore. Only then did he creep out of his hiding place.

It was only a few paces to the column. He knelt down at the foot of it and gingerly opened part of the wood paneling. This inconspicuous construction facilitated his further effort; he had worked on it by the glow of his flashlight for the past three nights until the early morning hours. Tonight he wanted to begin to hollow out the column, an equally arduous and time-consuming task. He carefully used his mason's chisel. The plaster could be removed without difficulty, bit by bit. He had set a schedule for all his preparations. He knew he had many nights ahead of him.

A week earlier, he had arrived in Munich. On his arrival, he had a porter bring him and his suitcases to Blumenstrasse, where he took up quarters with the Baumann family. He had received an offer from them in response to his ad in the *Münchener Zeitung*, which he had placed weeks earlier from Schnaitheim. The room on the third floor was not exactly inexpensive: The monthly rent was thirty-five reichsmarks, and breakfast was an additional twenty, but he accepted nonetheless. Time was running short. He had to get to Munich. His decision had to be put into action.

The Baumanns were approachable, friendly, and in no way intrusive. Not until two days after his arrival did they ask their tenant what he was doing in Munich. Elser told them that he was there to attend a polishing course, because that was a worthwhile additional skill for his occupation as a carpenter.

Though they noticed that in the first days Elser left his room only for meals and was often out at night, this apparently did not arouse their suspicion.

When they asked, I told them that I was pondering my invention at night and that I sat on a bench outside for that purpose, Elser later said. What his invention was did not seem to particularly interest the Baumanns. *I wasn't asked further questions about it.*

His daily routine proceeded according to a strict schedule: After breakfast, he retreated to his room to make further sketches and drawings. He was still working out unresolved details of his explosive device. In the afternoon, he occasionally helped Frau Baumann with the shopping, or he rested on the sofa for his nightly work. Around seven in the evening, he left his room on Blumenstrasse and headed to the Bürgerbräu Beer Hall.

When I worked at night in the Bürgerbräu Beer Hall, I always went between eight and ten o'clock to the restaurant of the Bürgerbräu for supper. I would sit at a table in the middle of the restaurant, eat à la carte, and have a glass of beer. I always paid around ten o'clock. I would then leave the restaurant, proceeding from there through the coatroom into the unlocked hall. In the beginning, the emergency lighting was on in the hall. Later—that is, after the outbreak of the war—there were no longer any lights on. At that time, there was only the light coming from the kitchen and the coatroom. I stayed in my hiding place until the hall was locked.

On the fourth evening after his arrival in Munich, Elser had already begun his work, as he later testified:

First I carefully removed the wooden strip on the baseboard of the paneling on the column, then the upper strip on the paneling—that is, I had to cut from the baseboard the strip that was milled on the upper part of the board, which was of one piece with the rest of the board. The upper strip was only a molding, which I could remove easily. That way I could saw out a piece of the column paneling so that after reattachment of the moldings, no saw cuts could be seen. I converted this cut-out board into a door by mounting pivot hinges on the top and bottom in the corner of the column. The other long side of the door board was not noticeable, because it overlapped with a natural joint with moldings milled on it. I attached a bolt to this door. Without removing any moldings or strips, I could open this bolt with a flat knife I could insert into the natural, vertical joint. Of course, in order to move the bolt from the outside, I had to cut the so-called tongue—that is, the protruding part of the adjacent board, which fit into the detached board under the molding.

It took me about three nights to make the door. That way, I could always begin my work immediately once I had opened the door, and at the end of my night's work I only had to close the door in order to conceal completely what was being done inside the column. Even if someone had looked at the column very closely during the day, he wouldn't have noticed any change to it at all. My work area was not blocked by tables or chairs, though there were some next to it.

Next Elser began to chip away at the side joints in order to remove the bricks bit by bit—an arduous task. He made only gradual progress, because he had to go about his work very carefully in order to make as little noise as possible.

I could only remove the bricks by using a brace and auger to drill holes close together in the brick joints filled with hard mortar, chipping away with the chisel at the mortar that remained, and then prying out the bricks with a longer chisel, bit by bit. Because rather coarse stones were contained in the mortar, which made a really loud noise whenever the auger struck them, I wrapped the back part of the auger in a piece of cloth and pressed firmly against the stone while working in order to somewhat muffle the sound. I wanted to prevent the noise to some extent, because the slightest sound echoed a great deal in the empty hall at night. I had to go about my work very carefully in general, and for that reason the work took a long time. I had to make sure with every break and with every turn of the auger to make as little noise as possible.

The fact that the toilet facilities in the Bürgerbräu Beer Hall automatically flushed every ten minutes was to his advantage. He used the few seconds during which the flushing broke the silence for a few forceful strokes of the chisel. Kneeling, repeatedly feeling around with his hands in the growing cavity, he worked for hours in the faint glow of his flashlight, which he had covered with a handkerchief in order to dim the light.

He caught the debris generated by chipping away at the bricks, the drill dust, and the stones in a sack he had made himself out of a towel, which he hung from a wire ring in the opening of the column. *When the bag was full, as it was relatively small, I emptied the contents into a cardboard box that could be closed with a cardboard cover. I always left this box in my hiding place on the gallery with the other boxes that were there.*

That night, Elser worked until half past two. Afterward, he put his tools into the opening of the column, closed the paneling, and neatly wiped up the remaining debris and dust that had fallen next to the bag. He went into his hiding place, took off his blue work pants, which he wore over his street clothes while he worked on the column, and left them in a corner of the room. He tried in vain to sleep for a few hours on the floor and waited until morning. As always, the doors to the hall were opened between seven and eight o'clock. He then left the hall, either through the coatroom or through the rear exit. At home, he retreated to his room; exhausted, he immediately fell asleep.

Not until the afternoon did he leave the apartment again with his brown suitcase, heading to the Bürgerbräu. Now he could enter the hall unhindered. Via the rear entrance, he proceeded to his hiding place in order to fetch the accumulated debris without drawing attention to himself. After a few minutes, he left the Bürgerbräu with the full suitcase and went down to the area behind the public bathhouse, where he dumped the debris into the Isar. He intended to remove the debris from the hall the same way in the weeks to come.

He then returned to Blumenstrasse, where he had things to do. *While I was working at night in the Bürgerbräu Beer Hall, I devoted myself during the day to the final exact design and construction of my machine.*

A complicated construction: Two built-in clocks were to set off the three explosive charges at a predetermined time. He had gone over the details of the plans again and again, rejecting, improving, and revising. Ultimately, he wanted his bomb to succeed so perfectly that its workings would astonish even the Gestapo.

Elser left nothing to chance, thinking everything through. During his work in the Bürgerbräu, a number of dances took place in the hall, which was often decorated for that purpose. To prevent the hollow space in the column's paneling from being discovered when nails were driven into it, he lined the wood on the inside of the door with a two-millimeter thick sheet of iron. That way, even if someone knocked on the column, the hollow space could not be discovered—another example of Elser's meticulousness.

Despite all his precautions, he was surprised once by a man when leaving his hiding place.

This man wanted to fetch a cardboard box from my hiding place and noticed me. After he had taken a box, he went away without saying anything to me and then came back onto the gallery with the manager. The man came from the left and the manager from the right. In the meantime, I had left my hiding place and taken a seat at a table on the eastern gallery, where, for the sake of appearances, I was writing a letter. When questioned by the manager, I explained to him that I had a boil on my thigh that I had wanted to squeeze. When he asked me what I was doing in the back room, I told him that I had wanted to open the boil there. I also told him that I had wanted to compose a letter at the table. The manager merely instructed me to write the letter in the garden, because I had no business being on the gallery. I then proceeded to the garden of the Bürgerbräu Beer Hall, where I had a coffee in order to avoid arousing suspicion. It was the same manager with whom I had already spoken on Easter in 1939.

Even though Elser had tried to get a job from him earlier that year, the manager did not seem to remember his face or the fact that because of this man he had admonished his busboy to stay out of personnel matters. Elser had never again heard anything about the busboy.

At home in his room in the Baumanns' apartment, Elser was safe from such unpleasant surprises, which endangered his plans. Nonetheless, he ended his stay with the Baumanns in late August. On September 1, a Friday, he moved into a new room, in the home of the Lehmann family in the Schwabing district, Türkenstrasse 94.

The room came to my attention through an ad in the Münchner Neueste Nachrichten, which I placed there at the end of August 1939. I had no previous acquaintance with the Lehmann family, just as I had had none with the Baumann family. There I had a small room for which I had to pay seventeen reichsmarks and fifty pfennigs, not including breakfast. As before, I registered my residence with the police under my real personal data and gave the Lehmann family information about my background and my profession when they asked. Once again, I told them that I was working on an invention and that I had moved to Munich for that reason, without providing further details. I continued to spend most of my time during the day in my room, leaving only to have lunch and dinner and to perform the preliminary work in the Bürgerbräu Beer Hall, which could be done only at night. Now and then, I also went to the Baumann family's home, where I chopped wood. For that, I received lunch, dinner, and some tip money. For the move I again used a porter, whose name I don't know. There, too, I kept my wooden suitcase locked all the time, so that no one could look inside of it.

The same day that Elser moved into the Lehmann family's home, a session began in the Berlin Reichstag at ten o'clock in the morning, in which Hitler—wearing a soldier's uniform—legitimized the attack against Poland, launched without a prior declaration of war.

In his speech, which was broadcast by all German radio stations, Hitler avoided the word "war." The goal of the invasion of Poland was solely to solve the problems of Danzig and to establish a "Polish Corridor." Hitler justified his attack on Poland as a response to the assault by Polish soldiers on the Gleiwitz radio station, which had in reality been staged by SD officers in Polish uniforms.

At the Lehmann family's home on Türkenstrasse in Schwabing, the voice of the Führer blared from the radio that morning.

Representatives, men of the German Reichstag, for months we have all been suffering from the agony of a problem that was bestowed on us by

127

the Versailles dictate and that, in its deterioration and degeneration,
has become unbearable to us. Danzig was and is a German city. The
Corridor was and is German . . .

I have therefore resolved to speak to Poland in the same language
that Poland has been using toward us for months . . .

Last night, for the first time, Polish regular soldiers fired on our own
territory. Since 5:45 AM, we have been returning fire.

Hitler was lying, but the German people burst into shouts of
"Sieg Heil!" Almost no one spoke of war, let alone an attack on
Poland; instead, it was solely a matter of the "active protection
of the Reich," as the invasion was called in a Wehrmacht report.
The Reich Propaganda Ministry had declared that there were to
be "no headlines in which the word war appears," and the Nazi-
coordinated press followed this policy.

On that day, Georg Elser was busy unpacking his suitcases in
his new room. He pushed his large wooden suitcase unopened
under his bed. In it were clock parts, clock weights, a shell case,
packets of powder, blasting caps and cartridges, various wires
and screws, and finally—underneath all that in the double
bottom—the last detailed drawing of his bomb. As always, he
kept the key to the wooden suitcase on him. He was happy with
the change of residence. He had more space to work and didn't
have to be mindful of the fine furniture as he had in the room
at the Baumanns'. Though the room was furnished simply and
functionally, it was sufficient for his plans, and the rent there was
half the amount it had been on Blumenstrasse.

Elser lay down on the narrow bed and looked out the large
window into the courtyard. He thought about Hitler's speech, to
which he had been able to listen only briefly. Invading Poland?
That was the beginning—that was war. At that moment, he was
convinced more than ever of the necessity of his attack. It had to
succeed—it was the only way to eliminate this bellicose leadership and prevent a war.

The days that followed confirmed his prognoses. On September 3, Ambassador Robert Coulondre delivered the French
declaration of war to German Foreign Minister Joachim von
Ribbentrop. France was thus at war with the German Reich. The

British government had already handed Ribbentrop a note in Berlin, threatening to fulfill the British obligation to Poland if the Germans were not *prepared promptly to withdraw their forces from Polish territory.*

The invasion of Poland and the declarations of war from France and Great Britain brought about abrupt changes in everyday life in the German Reich. As of September 1, a complete blackout was imposed and the public was instructed to take cover in bomb shelters when the air raid sirens sounded. No bombs were falling yet on the cities; it was still only British and French propaganda leaflets.

Starting in early September, anyone who listened to enemy radio stations was threatened with prison or the death penalty, because—according to the suspicions of the Nazi regime—every word was designed to "harm the German people." For the politically and racially persecuted, more than anyone, the outbreak of war meant new, escalating repressions: Jews were required to obey nightly curfews—in summer as of 9:00 PM and in winter as of 8:00 PM—and numerous unionists, social democrats, and communists were arrested as enemies of the state. By decree of the chief of the security police and the security service Reinhard Heydrich, anyone who publicly voiced doubts about a German victory could be "liquidated." But the National Socialists didn't need to worry, as the majority of the German people were still cheering, still raising their arms in the Hitler salute—there was still "one people, one Reich, one Führer."

* * *

Night after night, Elser was busy hollowing out the cavity in the column so that he could finally get the exact measurements he needed in order to finish his work on the explosive device. For that, he enlisted the help of craftsmen, commissioning several small jobs or buying material from them under the guise of working on an invention. He developed a closer relationship with Karl Bröger, a master carpenter who allowed him to work in his nearby workshop, where he built the case for his explosive device. Later Elser recalled: *Of course, as time went on, he often asked me what*

129

I was working on or why I needed this or that. I always told him it was an invention. When he asked further questions, I told him that it was a secret for the time being. When he asked later whether what I was making was the sort of alarm clock that also turned on a lamp when it went off in the morning, I said, "Yes, something like that."

Elser kept his contact with his landlords to a minimum. In the meantime, the Lehmanns had become accustomed to the somewhat strange habits of their tenant, such as his idiosyncrasy of always locking his room and the fact that he was never home at night. It must have been an unusual "invention" indeed that their taciturn tenant was working on. "Maybe he's not an inventor at all, but a crackpot," said Herr Lehmann, a practically minded man, who was a paperhanger.

"But he always pays his rent on time and is friendly and helpful," his wife replied. Both shook their heads. They couldn't figure out this Georg Elser . . .

In early October, when he had to spend a few days in bed because his right knee was extremely swollen and inflamed, Frau Lehmann had taken care of him, and Elser had groaned about being thrown off schedule with the preparations for his invention due to the ailment. He had been really nervous, she told her husband. When Elser gave notice in the middle of the month for November 1, informing them that he was returning to his hometown, the Lehmanns believed it had to do with the "invention." Perhaps, they thought, their tenant had not finished it. "He overextended himself, and now he has run out of money," Herr Lehmann scoffed.

On the afternoon of Saturday, October 28, Elser was lying in bed in his room, thinking about Elsa. He had written her only two letters from Munich, just a few lines of no consequence. He hadn't answered her letters. He knew that they had no future together. The attack lay ahead of him, the last decisive preparations—there was no space for Elsa. Was there space for anyone?

He had even lost contact with Eugen. The last time he had seen him had been in July in Königsbronn. On that occasion, he had met him with his wife, and they had spoken about his plans to go to Munich. They had also talked briefly about politics and the Nazi regime. The leadership had to be eliminated, Georg had blurted out, and Eugen had looked at him with surprise. Since then, they hadn't seen each other. In September, he had sent Eugen a letter with his Munich address and the request to pass it on to his father. He had not wanted to send it to him directly at home, lest his mother or his brother Leonhard find out his address.

Despite his difficult and often humiliating experiences with his father over the previous years, he had gravitated toward him ever since the quarrels over the inheritance of the house. His father had taken his side when he had decided to leave the house. He had broken off all contact with his mother and Leonhard. He kept in touch only with his sister Maria, who lived with her husband and her small son in Stuttgart. A few days earlier, he had written her a brief letter.

Dear sister, Karl and Franzle!

How are you doing? I will probably pay you a visit in early November. Please let me know whether you can use the following objects: suits, shirts, socks, sweaters, camera, two pairs of shoes, my carpentry tools, umbrella, three hats. Please let me know immediately whether you have a use for these things. With warm regards,

Georg

After a few days he received an answer. *I'm astonished at your letter. I don't understand it. I'm happy that you will visit me. These days, one can always use those things,* his sister wrote, asking in bewilderment: *Are you joining the military or going abroad?*

"Abroad," Georg thought, as he scanned the lines. "There's a long way to go before then. First the assassination—then the escape."

Evening was approaching. He felt lonely. He lived in a city that was foreign to him, where he knew no one. The psychological strain from the isolation during the attack preparations made it hard for him to speak to anyone. He was alone. In recent weeks, he had even attended a church service for the first time in a long time.

In the course of the year, I started going to church more often, perhaps about thirty times. Recently I have occasionally gone to a Catholic church on weekdays to say the Lord's Prayer, when there was no protestant church nearby. In my view, it doesn't matter whether you do this in a protestant or a Catholic church. I admit that these frequent church visits and prayers were connected with my deed, which was weighing on my mind, for I probably would not have prayed so much if I had not been preparing and planning the deed. It is true that I always felt somewhat calmer after praying.

With the help of his acquired piety, it was possible for him to draw strength for his plan. He was not a religious man, but his worldview was strongly influenced by Christian belief. *I believe that God created the whole world and human life. I also believe that nothing happens in the world without God's knowledge. People certainly have free rein, but God can intervene when he wants,* he later said during his interrogations.

The fact that God did not intervene at that time, that he stood idly by and did not simply end the war, that he tolerated a dictatorship and a cruel oppressive state—all this troubled Elser. His religious values foundered on social and political reality. Was there no right to resist—no duty to kill a tyrant like Hitler?

He pushed his doubts aside. *As to whether I regard the act I committed as a sin in terms of protestant doctrine, I would like to say, "In a deeper sense, no!" I believe in the continued life of the soul after death, and I also believe that I would go to heaven if I still had a chance to prove by my further life that I intended good. Through my deed, I wanted to prevent even greater bloodshed,* he later stated. Nonetheless, it can be gleaned from his remarks that he agonized for a long time over the thought that he might have to accept the deaths of innocent people. Would the bomb actually strike Hitler?

* * *

It was dark when Elser set off for the Bürgerbräu. In accordance with his nightly routine, he entered the Bräustüberl around half past eight, ordered his meal, and proceeded around half past ten through the coatroom into the hall. He went up onto the gallery to do the last work on the cavity he had chiseled into the column.

For the past several nights, he had worked on the opening until the early morning hours. He had to make up for the time he had lost because of his damaged knee, which still hurt. Alternately crouching and kneeling, he removed the last of the debris from the column. He was glad that he had finished the loud chiseling work some time ago, because ever since the beginning of the war, air raid guards were stationed in the small downstairs hall, the Alt-Münchener-Saal, and so he had to proceed especially quietly and inconspicuously. But the final masonry work presented no problems. Now the explosive device could be installed.

At 6:30 AM, he left his hiding place as usual through the rear exit, which led out onto Kellerstrasse. No one noticed the small man in the dark blue worsted suit, black shoes and a coffee-brown sweater.

When leaving the hall, in order to avoid arousing any suspicion, I never used particular caution. I always entered and left the hall only in the way I've described. I never broke in, Elser later explained under questioning.

It was a Wednesday, the first day of November, when he parted from the Lehmanns. He had packed up his things and stored them in Karl Bröger's workshop, which was in the back of a courtyard only a few houses down on Türkenstrasse. Elser brought the rest of his belongings—three suitcases and boxes full of linens and tools—to the main train station to send them to his sister Maria, whom he still planned to visit in Stuttgart before his escape to Switzerland.

That evening, he began the final, decisive preparations.

Once I had assembled everything, I tested the component parts, including the clocks, several times to make sure they were working properly—without, of course, installing percussion caps and blasting caps or explosives. At home that evening, I filled the explosive container with the explosives— that is, only with gunpowder—and screwed the lid shut. I then inserted the blasting cap into the hole, packed this explosive container as well as the detonation apparatus in my suitcase, and brought it to the Bürgerbräu. . . .

On the gallery of the hall, in the glow of my flashlight covered with a blue handkerchief, I opened in the usual way the door of the cavity I had made. I first placed the shell case, around which I had bound a metal frame at home, in the rearmost corner of the cavity. At home I had also fastened one of the filled clock weights onto the shell case with a metal strip, so that the second explosive container was on the shell case.

The next night, he filled the container with the explosives; he also planted the remaining gunpowder and explosive cartridges in the cavity. Once again, he was unobserved.

Finally, on the night of November 3, he wrapped the clocks in packing paper, tied them up carefully, and walked to the Bürgerbräu Beer Hall—but there was an unexpected complication. For some reason, the doors to the hall were locked. Where would he spend the night now? Because the storeroom of the carpenter's workshop was inaccessible to him due to a passage that Karl Bröger locked at night, Elser had only one choice: He slept in the garden of the Bürgerbräu Beer Hall, where the beer barrels were stored. Not until the next day, November 4, was he able to set to work installing the clocks in the column.

Because I knew that a dance was being held in the hall that evening, a Saturday, I entered the Bürgerbräu from Rosenheimer Strasse, bought a ticket, and proceeded to the gallery, where I put the clocks I'd brought with me in my hiding place. I took a seat on the gallery near the music podium and watched the dance from there. I had no company. At the end of the dance—this was on November 5, around one o'clock—I proceeded from my seat into my hiding place and waited there until the hall had been emptied and locked. By waiting about half an hour, I made sure that there was no one left in the hall. I then went to install the clocks in the column, but realized that the front area where the case was to be put in was too narrow. Although I chipped away at the front area, I did not manage to insert the clock case, so I closed the door again, packed up my clock, and waited for daybreak in my hiding place. Early in the morning, I left the hall by the side emergency exit near the kitchen, which had been unlocked in the meantime.

I went through the brewing facilities to Kellerstrasse and from there to Bröger's storeroom. There I rounded off the rear corners of the clock case by sawing and rasping. By my estimation, the clock case would now definitely fit into the front area of the cavity in the column of the Bürgerbräu.

This did not place his systematic plan in danger. The next evening, he returned to the Bürgerbräu with the wrapped-up clock cases. As on the evening before, a dance was being held in the hall. Once again, Elser bought a ticket and proceeded to the gallery.

That day the dance was over around midnight. After about an hour, I proceeded to the column from my hiding place, opened the door, and confirmed by inserting the clock case into the front area of the hollow that it now fit. I fastened the clock case with metal strips and then inserted wire ropes, which I had bound together slightly near their ends, into the eyelet of the retention bolt, tightening them by twisting the free end. Finally I had to restart the two clocks, which had of course stopped during the transport, and set the correct time by synchronizing them with a pocket watch. In order to do so, I opened the front of the clock case, which I had, as a precaution, converted into a door as well. Later I closed it again and let things run their course.

At six o'clock he was finished. He had finally done it. Three months had passed since he had begun to remove the first bricks from the column. For more than thirty nights, he had worked on the gallery of the Bürgerbräu Beer Hall—always by himself, always in the dark, always in danger of being discovered. Now he had achieved his goal.

As he left the hall that morning one last time through the side emergency exit near the kitchen, the psychic pressure drained away from him—at least for a few minutes. Feeling content, he went down to Isartorplatz to have a cup of coffee at a kiosk. From now on, the clock is running, he thought. From now on, the bomb is ticking that will shake Nazi Germany from its slumber. He took a hefty sip.

That same day, Georg Elser left Munich. Shortly before ten o'clock, wearing a gray-blue suit and a double-breasted coat, a gray hat on his head, he boarded the local train to Ulm. From there he would travel on to Stuttgart. As hand luggage, he carried a brown suitcase and two packages.

He took off his heavy coat, laid it carefully over the suitcase on the luggage rack, and took a seat. Shortly thereafter, the train began to move. Georg thought of his sister Maria. When had they last seen each other? She had been married to Karl for four years. After the wedding, he had helped the two of them set up their apartment. A gong rod on a grandfather clock had broken during the move, and he had repaired the clock. The last time he had seen Maria and Karl had been in January—he could no longer remember the exact date. They had been surprised when he had visited without any particular reason or advance notice. That weekend he had first taken the train to Esslingen, where he had met Elsa, who had in the meantime found work there. He had told her of his plans to go to Munich. She had asked him repeatedly why it had to be Munich, of all places. Because it was a beautiful city, he had answered untruthfully. They had spent the night at an inn near the train station, and he had known then that it would be their last night together. Afterward, he had traveled on to Stuttgart.

Georg had walked to Lerchenstrasse, where Maria lived with her husband, Karl, and their son, Franz. At the apartment, he had found only Karl and little Franz. Because her husband was unemployed, Maria had accepted a job in a clothing factory. Later they had taken a long walk together and picked up Maria from work. After dinner, Georg had gone back to Königsbronn. His sister had said to him: "Come visit us more often. Stuttgart isn't at the other end of the earth."

Now, ten months later, they would see each other again. Slowly, the train arrived in Stuttgart. The clock showed that it was almost half past two. Georg got off the train, brought his luggage to the storage facility, which was directly opposite the station, and walked across the square to the Württemberger Hof hotel to meet Karl, who had in the meantime found a job as a butcher there.

A hotel employee told me that his workplace was a few houses down on the same street. I found my brother-in-law busy with menial work, because he apparently didn't have much to do at the moment as a butcher. My brother-in-law accompanied me back to the train station, helped me pick up my luggage, summoned a porter with a three-wheeler, and then returned to his workplace. I rode with the porter on his vehicle to Lerchenstrasse 52, where I found my sister at home.

That evening, they sat together in the living room and talked about Königsbronn, their family, and the state of their father's health. "I want to go and see Father one more time," said Georg. "I want to visit the Sauler family in Schnaithaim one more time, too."

Maria and her husband made pensive faces. "Do you have to go abroad?" Maria asked.

"Yes, I have to go over the fence," Georg answered tersely. "Nothing can be done about it."

Neither his sister nor his brother-in-law asked any further questions. Didn't they want to know more? Georg assumed that Maria believed he planned to go abroad because of his alimony payments. The suspicion bothered him, but he didn't say anything.

Shortly thereafter, he retreated to the bedroom where Maria had made half of the marriage bed for him. Beforehand, Karl had said good-bye to him. "Thank you for the things; I'll take good care of them, and if you ever need anything, you can gladly have it back," he said, offering Georg his hand. Georg shook his head. "Go ahead and keep it—I won't need it anymore."

That day, Georg bequeathed all that he owned to his sister and his brother-in-law:

I gave everything in the suitcases, boxes, and packages to my sister and brother-in-law. In them were screws, nails, and tools with which I worked and built at home. In the large wooden box were my suits, clean underwear, [and] two half-finished clock cases, as well as a cardboard box containing three or four clock mechanisms. These were meant for table clocks. . . .

I opened the suitcase, the packages, and the boxes in the presence of my sister and brother-in-law. The two of them took the things into safe-keeping. I showed my sister the double bottom in the large wooden box. I merely unscrewed the double bottom and screwed it back down, without any further explanation.

The next morning, he had breakfast with Maria and his nephew in the kitchen. That day, his sister didn't go to the factory. Once again, they talked about Königsbronn and the family problems. They discussed how the conflict over the house had torn the family apart, and Georg confided in Maria about his deep-seated anger over the injustice he had suffered. He had broken

137

off all contact with their other siblings. "Either there is justice or there is none," he said to her. Maria nodded thoughtfully.

That afternoon, after a short walk, Maria accompanied her brother to the train station. The goodbye was brief. "Be well and don't forget to write," she said to her brother, giving him her hand. "All the best to you," Georg replied tersely. Then he boarded the train to Munich.

A few days earlier—while I was still in Munich, before leaving for Stuttgart—I had decided that I would return to Munich. Because I had finished installing the clocks two days later than I had originally planned, I was anxious to check again whether they might have stopped. After I had installed, restarted, and set the clocks on November 6, 1939, I had only half an hour before I had to leave the hall. But I wanted to be safe, and for that reason I went back to Munich.

Because he had only ten reichsmarks left from his savings, he had asked Maria at breakfast for fifteen reichsmarks, assuring her that he would pay the money back quickly. Maria had given him thirty instead.

Now, as the train headed toward Munich, he tried to close his eyes. He saw the column, the Führer—would the assassination succeed? Would the leadership be killed? Would his subsequent escape to Switzerland succeed?

I wanted to be in Switzerland before my clocks set off the explosion. Switzerland had seemed to me the most obvious choice. Other countries, such as Italy, would have been completely unfamiliar to me, but I knew the border crossing points to Switzerland near Konstanz very well from the several years I had lived in that area. Back then, however, I had never contemplated crossing the green border. That hadn't been necessary, because at the time I had been in possession of a local border-crossing pass. After starting the clocks and crossing the border illegally, I planned to look for work in Switzerland as a carpenter or some other sort of job. . . .

I also intended—and had already thought this through—to write the German police a detailed letter from Switzerland explaining that I alone was the culprit in the assassination and had no co-conspirators or confidants. I would have sent a precise drawing of my device as well as a description of the execution of the deed, so that my claims could have been verified. My sole aim in sending such a message to the German police was to ensure that absolutely no innocent parties would be arrested during the search for the perpetrator. I had also considered the possibility that I might be extradited from Switzerland to Germany. To prevent this from happening, I planned to take with me certain material that I believed would be of interest to the Swiss military.

When I worked in the shipping department of the fittings factory in Heidenheim, I had, in accordance with my duties, kept a notebook on deliveries, such as empty powder boxes that we had sent full to a certain company. Although the company had provided this book at that time, I took it home with me after the termination of my employment, because only a few pages had been written on. I no longer recall whether I had at that time considered the possibility that I could use these entries later.

When I left the company, the notebook was not demanded from me. I took it along with my other things to Munich on August 5 and continued to use it there for occasional entries. However, it was not the same notebook as the one in which I drew the sketch with the dimensions of the column during my Easter visit. It is possible that when I took the notebook with me to Munich on August 5, I did so with the idea already in mind that I could put the entries in it to use later in Switzerland. The pages I planned to take with me to Switzerland contained entries showing that a number of German companies were active in German armaments manufacturing. I firmly hoped that the Swiss would not expel me if I provided this information to them. If they had nonetheless deported me from Switzerland, I would have asked to be sent to France, though I had no particular reason for that either. I wanted only to pursue a steady job. I did not know that the French put so-called emigrants in concentration camps. With respect to France, I did not think of a reward either. I hoped only to receive a residence permit.

In the event of deportation, if the Swiss had not already taken from me the information about the German armaments companies, I would have given these notes to the French. I have to admit that I remember, when I entered the company or perhaps somewhat later, having been informed of the need for secrecy regarding all details about the powder factories. As far as I know, a piece of paper was presented to all of us at the time, which we had to sign. I no longer recall whether there was anything on it about treason, espionage, or the death penalty.

I had scarcely reckoned with the possibility that I would not manage to make it to Switzerland—that is, I firmly hoped that my escape would succeed. If they catch me, I thought, then I will just have to accept the punishment.

On the evening of November 7, around half past nine, Elser arrived in Munich. Because he only rarely read daily newspapers or listened to the radio, he could not have known that his plan was more than endangered.

The day before, the regional leadership of Munich-Upper Bavaria had announced that the annual commemorative program on November 8 in the Bürgerbräu Beer Hall was to be abridged due to the exigencies of the war. Instead of the Führer, his deputy Rudolf Hess would speak, and the commemorative march on November 9 would be canceled. Instead, a scaled-down wreath-laying ceremony was to take place. Today, on November 7, the *Völkischer Beobachter* disseminated this report.

Elser knew nothing of this as he walked through the large train station. Outside he boarded a streetcar heading toward the Bürgerbräu Beer Hall. He was carrying a package with a piece of sausage in it, and in his pockets he had a pocketknife, a pair of pincers, and various springs and screws, in case he should need them. It was about ten o'clock in the evening when he arrived at the Bürgerbräu.

Coming in by the main entrance on Rosenheimer Strasse, I went through the coatroom into the hall, which was empty and dark. I didn't notice anyone observing me. I saw no one. The door to the hall was not locked. In the hall, I proceeded immediately to the gallery and listened at the door of the column to check whether the clock mechanisms were still running. By pressing my ear against the door, I could hear the ticking of the clocks very faintly. I then opened the door with the pocketknife, opened the clock case, and made sure with my pocket watch that the clock mechanisms were not fast or slow. The clock was working properly.

Elser closed the paneling and retreated to his old nightly hiding place. After the doors to the hall were unlocked, he left as usual shortly after six o'clock in the morning through the side emergency exit.

Outside on Rosenheimer Strasse, a poster caught his eye and he went up to it. On it, THE FÜHRER SPEAKS was written in large print, and underneath those words was the event description: *Meeting of the "old fighters" on November 8 in the Bürgerbräu Beer Hall, Admission 6:00 PM—Music will be played by the marching band of the Adolf Hitler Standard.* Elser read the announcement twice, including the list of participating groups in small print: the "old fighters," the surviving comrades of the "sixteen fallen," the guests of the Führer, national and regional party officials, SA and SS officers, leaders of the Hitler Youth, and labor leaders.

Elser turned around and looked at the Bürgerbräu Beer Hall once again. At that moment a strange mood came over him. Was it pride and satisfaction? Was it loneliness and fear? He felt his heart racing, and in his brain the bomb ticked in sync with it. "It has to succeed," he said softly to himself.

Shortly before ten o'clock, he bought a third-class ticket at the train station counter for the route Munich-Ulm-Friedrichshafen-Konstanz. He took the local train to Ulm, where he transferred to the express to Friedrichshafen, arriving there at around six o'clock in the evening. Before the departure of the steamer to Konstanz, he had forty-five minutes, which he used to get a shave in a barbershop. While his face was lathered, he looked into the large mirror in front of him. The white foam had given him a mask, which felt for a moment like a soft, warm, protective covering. As the barber drew the razor through the foam with a practiced hand, the pleasant feeling swiftly abandoned Elser. He thought of the bomb, of his escape, of Switzerland—of tomorrow.

CHAPTER TWELVE

"Enhanced Interrogation"

As if given a sudden electric shock, Georg Elser shot up. Hands had seized him and yanked him out of his sleep. Was it a dream? The cell was dark, with only the searchlight from the yard drawing a vague silhouette of his plank-bed. He got up, felt his way to the sink three paces from the bed, and turned on the faucet. For a moment, he let the water run through his spread fingers, and then he splashed the tingling coldness on his face. Slowly, he turned around. His thoughts crept along the walls, images bored into his brain: the arrest at the border, the interrogations in Konstanz and Munich, the transfer here to the Gestapo headquarters in Berlin, hours of questioning, the same questions, the same answers, again and again.

He sat down on the bed. He found it hard to breathe. A mountain of despair, guilt, and anger seemed to be crushing him.

* * *

Berlin, Prinz-Albrecht-Strasse 8. This center of the planning and management of National Socialist terror—where desk perpetrators focused on the "proper implementation" of "procedures" and typically stayed away from the actual sites of horror—was at the same time a place where people were beaten and tortured. In their offices on the upper floors, the Gestapo conducted "enhanced interrogations"—*verschärfte Vernehmungen*, as the torture methods were called in German bureaucratese. The victims included communists, social democrats, unionists, and members or supposed members of resistance organizations, as well as those who refused to accept the legitimacy of Nazi state power, such as Jehovah's Witnesses or individual representatives of the churches. The interrogations were humiliating, tormenting, and—at times—deadly. Those interned in the in-house prison, as Georg Elser was, had to fear for their lives.

At nine o'clock in the morning on Wednesday, November 22, the two bolts on Elser's cell door slid back noisily. The door opened to reveal a Gestapo officer, whose terse order rang out loudly. "Elser, come with me!" The officer was wearing a uniform and standing in the doorway with his legs spread and his hands clasped behind his back. At his left side stood another uniformed man, leaning his shoulder against the wall and eyeing Elser impassively. Without saying a word, they walked through long, wide corridors and climbed stairs, until they stood outside the interrogation room. By now, Elser recognized the door, which led straight into the heart of terror. Inside, his tormentors were already waiting, preparing to continue the "enhanced interrogations." It was their job, and they performed it as was expected of them.

The door flew open. *He had a shaved head and a completely swollen face,* his sister Maria later recalled of her brother's appearance. Had the Gestapo henchmen mauled Georg so badly in order to finally compel her to confess that she had known about his assassination plans? She had already been interrogated many times over the past several days—alone, with her husband, and in the presence of her brother. Always the same questions: "Did you know about it? Were you in contact with your brother? Didn't he visit you before his escape attempt? Didn't he tell you anything? Didn't you have any suspicions?"

At times the Gestapo officers would be cold and aggressive, while at other times they would package their questions in friendly phrases. There was method in everything. Maria and her husband always gave the same answers. "No, we didn't know anything about it! No, we didn't notice that! No, we had nothing to do with the attack!"

They had already explained all that after their arrest in Stuttgart, but no one believed them. Their apartment was searched, they were interrogated again and again, and ultimately they were brought to Berlin on a special train. *I spent the train ride in a compartment with my husband, guarded by two police detectives,* Maria later recalled. *During the whole journey, I did not get to see any of my family members. In Berlin, I was first brought to the Moabit prison and several days later to the Hotel Kaiserhof. After several days, my family members were permitted to return home, but my husband and I were put in the Moabit prison again.*

The two of them would be detained in Berlin longer than all the other family members. The Gestapo officers used every means at their disposal to pry a confession out of them, but their efforts were in vain. She and her husband had to pay a high price for their perseverance: They would not be released from prison until February 18, 1940, after countless, grueling interrogations.

On that Wednesday morning, Maria still suspected nothing of the long ordeal ahead of her. For ten days, they had been in this city, of which they had seen only the prison, the hotel, and the offices of the Gestapo. She had already been confronted with Georg three times—but this time was the worst.

The Gestapo torturers demonstrated cruelly what they understood by "enhanced interrogation." But what did they expect to achieve? Georg had long since confessed, providing minutely detailed testimony on his plan, the preparations and the execution of the attack. Did they still believe in a plot, in masterminds and string pullers? Did they think that the whole Elser family was in on a conspiracy against the Nazi regime?

Maria had the impression that the Gestapo officers were trying to extract a confession from her by force. Why else would they have abused her brother so badly the previous night in order to confront her now with his miserable condition? One of their objectives was fulfilled, however: Maria suffered a nervous breakdown.

Georg's mother, too, was at the end of her strength. She and her husband had already been questioned incessantly in Stuttgart. Now, in Berlin, they had to submit to severe interrogations once again. She later recalled her reunion with her son.

In Berlin, I was first brought to a prison and locked up, and then the interrogations began. There, too, I was questioned every day, almost always by a different officer. At one point, I was led into a large room where my son Georg was sitting at a long table. He wept when I was brought in to him. I was seated opposite him and was asked whether this was my son Georg and whether I believed that he had carried out the attack. I again expressed my conviction that I did not believe that he had done a thing like that. I didn't speak to Georg himself, because I didn't know whether I was permitted to speak to him or not, so I didn't dare to say anything to him.

Every day the family members were interrogated, often for hours on end—sometimes in a kind tone, other times in a harsh tone, sometimes by one Gestapo officer, other times by two or as many as four. At one point, an interrogation took place in which everyone had to participate. They sat at a large table and were questioned as a group. Everyone was relieved when it was finally over and they were brought back to the Hotel Kaiserhof.

Georg's mother later described the circumstances in the hotel: *We family members each got a room of our own. We got proper meals, but were not allowed to leave our rooms. In the hallway outside our rooms, some police officers were always on patrol so that we could not leave. In the hotel, we were then allowed to meet again during the day and eat meals together as a family. At night, we went back to our separate rooms.*

Georg's sister Friederike and her husband, Willy, were arrested in Schnaitheim and were initially detained and interrogated in Stuttgart. From there they were ultimately sent on to Berlin for the Gestapo interrogations. Later Friederike recalled those life-altering days.

My husband and I first learned of the attack in the Bürgerbräu Beer Hall on November 9 from a report on the radio. Beforehand we had known nothing about Georg considering such plans or intending to commit an assassination attempt on Hitler. That evening, a description of the suspected perpetrator was broadcast on the radio. I told my husband that you might almost think it was Georg, as he fit the description. The next morning, three detectives came from Stuttgart, arrested my husband and me, and brought us to Heidenheim. Our house was searched, but nothing was found or taken from the premises. Toward evening, we were brought in a car from Heidenheim to Stuttgart, where I was locked up in the prison on Büchsenstrasse. There was no room for my husband in the car, so he wasn't brought to Stuttgart until the next day. In Stuttgart, I was separated from my other family members and did not see them at all. I was locked up there for about ten or twelve days and interrogated every day, sometimes even at night. During the interrogations, I still wasn't told what was actually going on and could not imagine what this was all about. I was questioned about my brother, and the officers wanted to know everything in precise detail—about his earlier life, with whom he had associated, and so on.

From Stuttgart, I was then transferred to Berlin, together with my husband, my mother, and my siblings. In Berlin, we were brought to Gestapo headquarters, to the Hotel Kaiserhof, where each of us got a room. We were treated well there, were given good food, and had no complaints. We were, however, strictly guarded by police detectives and Gestapo officers. We were in Berlin another six or seven days, during which we were often interrogated. In Berlin, too, I was asked the same questions again and again—about my brother Georg's whole life from childhood on. We were also asked whether we had known anything about the attack, but I couldn't provide anything but the truth and had to say that I had no idea about that matter. After six or seven days, we were all released, with the exception of my sister Maria, who was kept there longer. Upon our release, we were presented with a document, which each of us had to sign, barring us from revealing anything about this matter or talking about it with other people.

This fact was later corroborated by Georg's brother Leonhard, who had also been brought to Berlin for the Gestapo interrogations with his wife, Erna. *Upon our release, we were expressly prohibited from saying anything about this matter.*

* * *

Besides Georg's family members, among those interrogated in Berlin was a young woman who had for a long time played a central role in his life—his former lover Elsa Heller. On that wet, gray Wednesday, they saw each other for the first time in ten months. Years later, Elsa recalled their last encounter.

147

He sat in the middle of the room on a chair, and I would definitely not have recognized him as my former lover in that condition. His face had been beaten until it was swollen and blue. His eyes protruded from their sockets, and he made a terrible impression on me. His feet, too, were swollen, and I think that he was sitting on a chair only because he could barely stand anymore. . . .

Before the end of the confrontation, a detective told me that I could now ask Elser something myself. But I could only ask, "Georg, did you do it?" At first, he did not answer, but only gave me a look that I will never forget. Then he opened his mouth very slowly and said, "Elsa." At that same moment, he received a blow to the neck from the officer standing behind him and was no longer permitted to speak. At the time, I was already firmly convinced, and remain so to this day, that he had wanted to say he was innocent. As his former lover, I could gather that much from his expression and his gestures.

Completely distraught, Elsa left the interrogation room on that afternoon of November 22. Gestapo officers brought her back to the Hotel Kaiserhof, where she was kept under special guard. She later said:

The doors were always locked, and guards stood outside them. I saw none of the members of the Elser family, who were also being held in this hotel. From occasional statements and from the behavior of the officers interrogating me, I concluded that I was apparently considered a particularly suspicious person along with Elser. They simply did not want to believe me when I said that I had no connection with Elser and knew nothing about the attack.

The Gestapo officers still refused to believe that Elser was the lone perpetrator, despite the fact that he had confessed and had sketched the design of the explosive device and made a model before their eyes. Plus, all the information he had provided in the interrogations up to that point had checked out. Could he really be a lone perpetrator—a man without conspirators, confidants, or ringleaders, unaffiliated with a resistance group or underground organization? He had been interrogated for hours, day and night. The previous evening, his questioners had finally lost patience. They conducted "enhanced interrogation"—but the slim man with the Swabian dialect only repeated that he had told them everything and did not know anything else. Not even a last confrontation with his sister Maria and his former lover Elsa had made him any more talkative. The idea that seeing Elser's wretched appearance would make one of the women reveal additional information had not panned out. But tomorrow was another day, and the Gestapo officers planned to turn the oppositional lone perpetrator into a *remorseful member of the people's community (Volksgemeinschaft)*. They had mastered the necessary methods for that. It was their trade.

The heavy door was forcefully closed and bolted. Elser lay down on the plank-bed. He was freezing, weak, and miserable. The dirty walls framed his field of vision. By now, he knew every mark, every scratch, and every tiny crack. The walls struck him as menacing; it seemed to him as if they were in league with his tormentors. Why didn't they offer him any protection? Why wasn't he safe from the grasping hands, the beating fists—not even here in his cell? Elser was tired. The long interrogations, as well as the confrontations with Maria and Elsa, had worn him out. His exhaustion had reached the stage when the senses rebel one last time against sleep and are momentarily reactivated. "Hopefully, this will all be over soon," he murmured, and then his head flopped to the side.

* * *

Not far from the in-house prison of the Gestapo, four men in customs uniforms were entering the Reich Finance Ministry. Xaver Reitlinger—the customs officer who had arrested Georg Elser attempting to escape to Switzerland on the evening of November 8—and his three colleagues—the young Zapfer, the head guard Trabmann, and the customs inspector Straube—had been invited to the evening reception. State Secretary Reinhard, also in uniform, praised the four men from Lake Constance, "You have done a great service to customs. We cannot thank you enough." Then he shook each of their hands, pinned the customs and border protection badge of honor on their uniforms, and presented them with a monetary reward. In recognition of their "exemplary professional ethos," they were also promoted: Zapfer to customs assistant, Reitlinger from customs assistant to customs inspector, Trabmann from secretary to inspector, and Straube from customs inspector to customs administrator. All four of them were extremely proud.

Afterward, during a round of drinks, the state secretary took Reitlinger aside. "I have seen to it that you will give a talk at the customs school about the arrest," he told him, and it sounded like an order.

Confused, Reitlinger replied, "But isn't it a state secret? The Gestapo in Karlsruhe forbade us to talk about it."

Reinhard put his hand on Reitlinger's shoulder. "Yes, but you are permitted to speak in front of comrades. You know that the SS is eager to take over customs, so now is the time to show your colors. After all, it was you and your colleagues who seized the assassin—and not the SS."

The next day, Reitlinger gave a brief talk in front of over a hundred customs candidates. He had quickly composed notes for it the previous night in the hotel. He did not feel comfortable in his own skin. Ultimately, he thought, it had only been a normal arrest. Who could have known that the illegal border crosser was the Bürgerbräu assassin?

No, he wasn't really a hero. He had done his duty and nothing more. Granted, he was somewhat proud. The latest edition of the *Völkischer Beobachter* lauded the vigilance of the Konstanz quartet and even ran a photo of him and his colleagues with State Secretary Reinhard. That afternoon, Reitlinger bought two copies of the newspaper. "A great memento of Berlin," he said to Zapfer, who was equally proud of the article.

That evening, the two of them had to report to Prinz-Albrecht-Strasse. Once again, Gestapo officers would question them on the events at the border. It quickly became clear to Reitlinger that they faced an entirely different reception from the Gestapo than they had from customs. Here it was of no interest to anyone that they had been promoted and praised for their work and decorated with a medal; here all that mattered were facts, additional information. Reitlinger was to answer the questions—nothing else. He later recounted:

It was in the Reichssicherheitshauptamt. I entered an office in which there were a few men in civilian clothing; I assumed they were senior officers of the security service. Here I was again questioned about the whole process of Elser's arrest. As during my earlier interrogations in Konstanz, I couldn't provide any further information. I had the impression that I was being pressed into the role of the accused. Here, too, I had to sign my statement. Zapfer was questioned separately from me. Afterward we compared notes on our interrogations, and I learned that he had experienced the interrogation tactics the same way I had.

After the interrogation, they were informed that SS-Führer and police chief Reinhard Heydrich also wanted to speak to them. "I am happy to be able to receive you," he greeted Reitlinger and Zapfer in his huge office. Then his expression became more serious.

Heydrich swore us to secrecy with a handshake regarding everything we knew about Elser's case. He said explicitly that we were accountable for that. We had to pledge our discretion to him with a handshake.
Thus Reitlinger later described the brief meeting with Heydrich.

It was dark when the two of them left the Reichssicherheitshauptamt, accompanied by two Gestapo officers. As they went downstairs to the waiting car, which would bring them back to the hotel, Reitlinger thought for a moment about the man he had arrested at the border. He must have been confined somewhere in this building, waiting for his interrogations in a cell of the in-house prison. Reitlinger wouldn't have wanted to be in his shoes. Undoubtedly, he would be indicted, and the justice system would make short work of a man who had tried to kill Hitler: Death penalty!

No, he really wouldn't want to change places with the fellow. He must be a madman, a fanatic, or a hired assassin. Reitlinger suspected the last of these.

Zapfer roused him from his thoughts. "Xaver," he said to him, "tonight we'll drink some wine and tomorrow we'll head home." Reitlinger nodded: "Thank God."

While the Konstanz quartet was celebrating its imminent departure from the capital of the Reich over drinks that evening, Gestapo officers were fetching Georg Elser from his cell. The fact that interrogations did not begin until late in the evening was neither unusual nor a matter of chance, but rather by design. The subjects fought against their exhaustion; lack of focus caused them to make careless statements; their power of resistance flagged. The Gestapo officers took advantage of this situation. Elser, too, had often been questioned at night. The interrogations frequently lasted into the morning hours. Now, as the hands of the clock moved to midnight, he had trouble following his guards. The imprisonment, the interrogations, the abuses had worn him down. Elser was a broken man.

The door to the interrogation room was opened. The guards escorted him to the middle of the room. "Sit down on that chair," a voice ordered harshly from the background. Elser looked at a small projection screen that had been set up in front of the filing cabinets. "Lights out," the voice ordered. On the screen flickered images of the funeral for the victims of the Bürgerbräu attack, who had been buried in Munich on November 11 in a state ceremony. Seven coffins were flanked by honor guards; before them was a sea of flowers and wreaths. The camera panned over to the family members—close-ups of weeping faces. "I didn't want that . . ." Sobbing, Elser broke down under the impact of the images.

"Lights!" commanded the voice, which belonged to a tall Gestapo officer who now emerged from the darkness and walked over to the desk. He nodded authoritatively to another officer, who planted himself next to Georg. The transcriber reached for his pencil.

> *Question:* *What were you thinking when you inspected your work and closed the doors for the last time on the night of November 7?*
>
> *Answer:* *I can no longer recall.*
>
> *Question:* *How had you imagined the outcome of the attack at that time?*
>
> *Answer:* *I had thought about that several times beforehand.*
>
> *Question:* *Did you think that a number of people might be killed?*
>
> *Answer:* *Yes.*
>
> *Question:* *Did you want that? And whom were you targeting?*
>
> *Answer:* *Yes. I was targeting the leadership.*
>
> *Question:* *Was that your objective throughout the whole preparation and implementation of the deed, or did you have doubts occasionally about what you were doing?*

Answer: *(After a long pause for thought) I no longer recall whether I had doubts or not. But I don't think I had any.*

Question: *How do you view today what you have done, after your plan failed and you killed eight people?*

Answer: *I would no longer do it.*

Question: *That is not an answer to my question.*

Answer: *The goal was not achieved.*

Question: *So are you indifferent to the fact that you caused the deaths of eight people?*

Answer: *No, I am not indifferent to that.*

Question: *What would you do if you were released today for some reason?*

Answer: *I would try to make up for what I've done wrong.*

Question: *How?*

Answer: *By trying to find my place and take part in the people's community.*

Question: *Could you do that?*

Answer: *I have changed my views.*

Question: *Because you were captured?*

Answer: *No, I believe firmly that my plan would have succeeded if my views had been correct. Because it did not succeed, I am convinced that it was not supposed to succeed and that my views were wrong.*

The last interrogation took less than half an hour. Shortly thereafter, the typewritten transcript was available. An officer gave it to Elser, who only skimmed the text. He was incapable of reading the content. On the last line were the words *Read, approved, and signed.* The transcriber handed him a pen. Without a word, he signed.

When SS-Gruppenführer Heinrich Müller read through the extensive interrogation transcripts the next day, he felt conflicted. On the one hand, as the person responsible for the investigations, he could be satisfied with the work of his officers. On the other hand, there was the fact that, despite "enhanced interrogations," this Elser had stood by his earlier testimony. It was not only in light of propagandistic considerations that the Nazi regime would be dissatisfied with the results, he knew. Of what use was the fact that the assassin had ultimately been overcome by doubt about the rectitude of his actions? Hitler, Himmler, and Heydrich clung to their "mastermind theory," and wanted proof that the British secret service stood behind the attack, but the results of the investigation provided no support for that at all. Along with a brief memorandum, Müller passed on the investigation results to the Nazi leadership. A few days later, he received a call from Heydrich. "The Führer has ordered that the trial shall take place only after the war, in order to demonstrate what perfidious methods the secret service has employed."

Elser became a prisoner in protective custody of the Reichssicherheitshauptamt. In a show trial, he would testify as the key witness against the British secret service. By then, thought SS officer Müller, we will certainly have prepared the fellow . . .

A few hours after Heydrich's phone call, a gray car stopped in the yard of Prinz-Albrecht-Strasse 8. Two Gestapo officers fetched Elser from his cell. "Where are we going?" he asked, as the Gestapo officers led him through the long corridors of the main prison.

"We're taking a trip," one of the officers answered. Amused, the other added, "Yes, to a camp." Their laughter resounded through the corridor.

CHAPTER THIRTEEN

The Death of Protective Custody Prisoner E.

Franz Fachner was a tall, slender man, who wore his blond hair severely parted and had alert blue eyes. In May 1939, he had been drafted into the Wehrmacht. The superior officers were struck by the young recruit's downright exemplary "Aryan" appearance. After only four weeks, he was transferred to a newly established "SS Police Division," which was made up of active police forces and was considered an elite troop. Its members were tall, young men "of German appearance," who were well trained in police service and intended for special missions on the front.

Fachner participated in the French campaign; after that, it was on to Russia. As a member of an assault squad at Leningrad during the first hard winter of 1941, at forty-five degrees below zero, he was seriously injured. For a year, he was in the hospital, but he never truly recovered. His right arm remained paralyzed.

Despite his injury, the SS found a use for him. After a long recovery period, he was transferred to Munich. At the Freimann barracks, Fachner got a new uniform and was told the name of his new place of operation: the Dachau concentration camp.

On the outskirts of Munich, Dachau was the first "official" camp established by the National Socialists. On the grounds of a former munitions factory, five thousand people would be interned. Dachau served as a model for camps that followed. Here the Nazis

155

tested all the nuanced methods of suppression and elimination of political and ideological opponents that they would later employ in the other camps. Dachau became the "primary school" of the SS: The majority of camp leaders who spread fear and terror for years in Germany and the occupied territories had passed through Dachau. Here they had all learned their bloody trade.

Fachner was detailed to guard the prisoners. At first, he felt uncomfortable with the idea of doing his service in a concentration camp. He had already heard some things about the camp. On March 22, 1933, it had been "put into operation," an older SS man informed him. From the first day on, Hitler's threat to do away with his political opponents after coming to power had been carried out here. Almost all communists who could be caught were sent to Dachau. Unionists and social democrats followed, and shortly thereafter, Jewish citizens as well. When prominent newcomers arrived at the camp, the SS guards came up with a "special program" for each of the prisoners to humiliate and torture them.

Political functionaries had to wear signs around their necks designating them as an "empty talker" or a "traitor to the workers;" others had to run the gauntlet in front of uniformed SS men who burst into laughter and jeering; academics were assigned to the hardest physical labor in the knowledge that they would soon collapse because they were unaccustomed to it. Many did not survive these harassments and died agonizing deaths.

From the beginning—later in increasingly perverse forms—there was in Dachau a *Strafkompanie,* a division of prisoners condemned to penal labor, which after 1940 was housed in two special blocks. These blocks were separated from the rest of the camp by barbed wire. The treatment there was particularly brutal, the food even worse than in the rest of the camp. There was also the so-called "bunker," a building with dark, musty cells in which prisoners had to spend months, often chained to the walls. The "standing cells" there were a particularly harrowing invention of the SS: On a square no more than two feet wide, prisoners were forced to spend their detention standing for days. It was to this camp that Fachner reported for duty in the summer of 1944, at a time when Dachau was completely overcrowded.

Beginning in 1939, the prisoner transports reflected the fascist politics of conquest. Besides prisoners from Germany, the camp registers listed mainly Polish, Soviet, Hungarian, Czech, and French inmates. From Poland, whole university faculties had been transported to Dachau in the course of the eradication of the Polish intelligentsia ordered by the National Socialist regime. From France came many resistance fighters, whose ultimate fate—like that of thousands of other prisoners—was known to no one.

The camp had expanded considerably over the previous years, mainly through the forced labor of the inmates themselves. Despite the expansion, the camp was hopelessly overcrowded. Often three or more prisoners shared the wooden frames designated as "beds"; inadequate nutrition and hygiene bred illnesses and epidemics. Documents would later reveal that in 1944 alone, over 30,000 people were imprisoned in the main camp—a camp that had initially been designed for 5,000 prisoners.

Fachner stood outside the camp gate and showed his papers unprompted. The guard on duty waved them away almost indifferently and then escorted him to the commandant's office. It was only a few hundred yards away. Fachner saw the electrically charged fence and behind it the rows of uniform barracks—the actual camp.

A senior officer greeted him. "So there you are. You are a man of many distinctions. I welcome you. Yesterday something crazy happened here. One prisoner ran amok, then another. It was a terrible day for us. We had to hang some of them. But don't be surprised. You'll see all sorts of things. Now read this through,"—he pressed a document about secrecy into his hands—"and then sign it."

Fachner was too excited to understand the text he read. His eyes darted over the paper, and then he signed.

"You will be in the censorship office," the SS man went on. "There you have to censor the prisoners' letters, all the letters coming in and out. For example, the prisoners are not permitted to receive razor blades or photos of their family members in the letters. Above all, they are not permitted to write negatively about the Dachau camp. Be attentive."

For four weeks, Fachner inspected the prisoners' incoming and outgoing mail. His colleagues, mostly older SS men, did their work routinely and emotionlessly. They had long ceased to take note of the fact that the letters were written by people in distress and fear. All that mattered to them was their own security, not other people's fates.

Then, on a Thursday, Fachner was instructed to report to a lieutenant on the second floor. The uniformed man had a close-cropped mustache and deep-set eyes. He greeted Fachner and said, "Come with me," beckoning him to follow. They left the building in which the censorship office was housed and walked the few yards to the actual camp gate. They went through the gate, crossed a small open area, and turned right, passing countless barracks, behind which guard towers rose at regular intervals. The lieutenant stopped in front of a heavy iron gate. "Do you see the prison building over there?" he asked Fachner, pointing to a one-story, long, stone building with barred windows. "Starting today, you'll be working there."

In the days that followed, his new superior, a perpetually grumpy SS-Obersturmführer, gave him a camp key with which he could also open all the cell doors.

Fachner was responsible for the wing for so-called "prominent prisoners." Two longtime inmates were assigned to him as helpers. Both were Jehovah's Witnesses who had been sent to the camp for "religious opposition." In the wing, Fachner was confronted with people who had been classified by the National Socialists as opponents, collaborators, and conspirators despite their prominent political, social, or economic positions and were now being kept in "protective custody"—often under privileged circumstances. Thus the former Austrian Chancellor Schuschnigg lived with his wife and daughter Sissy in two cells; the former Reichsbank President Schacht did not have to go without his customary high, stiff collar here; and the geopolitician Karl Haushofer could not complain about a lack of technical literature. Military officers in disfavor—such as the former General Staff Chief Halder or the military commander of Belgium, General von Falkenhausen—were under Fachner's supervision, as were church dignitaries. The abbot of the Metten Abbey, a Greek archbishop, Pastor Martin Niemöller—they had all been interned in the camp as members of the opposition. They could only speculate on their ultimate fate. Even the Nazis were still indecisive about what should happen to many of their prominent prisoners: long-term isolation or extermination?

In the meantime, Fachner had come to terms with the terror system. Sometimes he had quiet doubts, when he thought about what was done to people in the camp: humiliation, torture, execution by firing squads, or hanging. Death was part of everyday life in Dachau. In the crematorium, death commandos performed horrific work around the clock. In special departments, medical experiments were conducted: People were infected with malaria or put in tubs full of ice water for hours in order to observe what stresses a human body could endure. The death of experiment subjects was factored in from the beginning. What counted here as a human life?

Fachner pushed aside any doubts that arose. After all, it was wartime, he reassured himself; drastic measures had to be taken, as his superiors had always told him. "You can't make an omelet without breaking eggs," was the word among the camp guards, and by broken eggs, they meant death—thousands of deaths. Actually, Fachner was glad to work in the so-called *Kommandanturarrest*, a "little camp" within the camp, where there were "special conditions" for the prominent prisoners. Perhaps they will be put on trial after the war, thought Fachner. That's for the regime to decide, not us. It was not his job to think about it. He was only doing his duty—nothing more.

On an ice-cold Wednesday, four SS guards brought a small, inconspicuous man to him in the *Kommandanturarrest*. "A transport from Sachsenhausen. You will get a phone call shortly," one of the four said before they left. Fachner led the new arrival to the guardroom. The telephone rang. "The new prisoner will get cell number six. You'll be given all further information later," the voice commanded brusquely. By now, Fachner had gotten used to the rude tone that prevailed among the camp management. Language had adapted to the system—it was efficient; there was not one word too many. Orders came tersely and aggressively, usually loudly and clearly. There was a lot of contempt and cynicism in the words, especially when they were directed at prisoners.

Fachner brought the man to cell number six. He looked ill. His face seemed sunken, his body emaciated. A wreck, thought Fachner. "What's your name?" he asked the prisoner.

The answer came softly and hesitantly: "Elser . . . Georg Elser."

Fachner opened the cell door with his large key and said: "I'll have you brought to me later to take down your information."

But that would not be necessary. Shortly thereafter, Fachner found out that the inconspicuous prisoner in cell six was the man who had carried out the attack on the Führer in the Bürgerbräu Beer Hall. He was informed that Elser had been interned for the past five years as a "special prisoner of the Reichssicherheitshauptamt" in the Sachsenhausen concentration camp.

In 1939, after the interrogations were concluded, the Gestapo had brought him there, twenty miles north of Berlin. The camp guards had regarded the slight man with the Swabian dialect as a good-natured fellow, a reserved, quiet prisoner, who never complained, rebelled, or caused trouble. He could be found every day in his small camp workshop, which had been set up for him in accordance with instructions from Berlin. Elser had become a heavy smoker over the previous years, but cigarettes were in short supply. To have them was like having cash, for cigarettes had long ago become the unofficial camp currency. Supervisors paid him with them for small jobs: bookshelves and chairs, drawers and candlesticks, which Elser made for them now and then in his workshop.

Smoking became the only pleasure that remained for him besides playing the zither. He submitted to his fate without complaints—a broken, lonely man, a prisoner whose "special purpose," in the view of the Nazi rulers, was yet to come, a prisoner under special protection—a dubious protection, to be sure. Sometimes he felt like a bird locked up in a luxurious cage. His cell was three times larger than the usual size and contained his small workshop; he got better food than the other camp inmates; and his guards had instructions to treat him well. However, the special treatment also included complete isolation from the other prisoners, as well as permanent supervision by two guards assigned to stay in his cell around the clock.

Elser was the best-guarded prisoner in the Sachsenhausen camp—a prisoner without a chance of release, without a future, completely cut off from the outside world. Even the rare letters he had written to Maria and Elsa remained unanswered. They had been confiscated in the Reichssicherheitshauptamt in Berlin along with the mail addressed to him.

That afternoon, Fachner did not have to fill out the usual obligatory file card for his new prisoner, who had been brought from Sachsenhausen to Dachau, as had other prominent prisoners, because of the advance of the Russian Army. "He is under the direct authority of the Gestapo in Berlin," the Obersturmbannführer had told him; therefore the man had to be guarded particularly carefully. "We don't want him doing something to himself and then it's our mess and we get the blame."

Fachner found his superior's concern somewhat excessive—almost cynical, in light of the daily murders in the camp. A human life was not worth anything here unless it was in some way useful to the system—even if only as a tragic figure in a show trial. The prisoners held in the protective custody cells had one thing in common: They did not have to fear death in the immediate future; their status guaranteed them survival for the time being in the midst of the machinery of death.

As in Sachsenhausen, a workshop was set up for Elser in his Dachau cell. During the day, he again did carpentry jobs for the camp management with the same care and meticulousness that had always distinguished his work.

In the evening, he played his self-made zither. The songs that came from his cell sounded heavy and melancholy. Sometimes Fachner sat down with him, watched him over his shoulder, and enjoyed the Viennese melodies; he had grown as fond of them as his prisoner was. Sometimes they got into a conversation and talked about music. Fachner had promised to get Elser some sheet music. They rarely spoke about politics, still less about the war, and not at all about the conditions in the camp. As an inmate, Elser was not permitted to speak about such subjects; as a concentration camp guard, Fachner was strictly forbidden to discuss them with prisoners. He knew that, but who adhered to official regulations at that time? Each of his colleagues was a master of life and death, an absolute ruler of the small domain under his control. Fachner knew many who took excessive advantage of that role. They fancied themselves "living devils" and recognized no laws other than their own.

The camp system endorsed their brutality, their unrelenting destructive impulses. The radical contempt for humanity among individual guards conformed seamlessly to a total system of state terror. Fachner was part of this murderous system. He attempted repeatedly to soothe his conscience with the fact that he did not personally participate in the machinery of death and spared the prisoners under his control beatings and torments. He made an effort to behave "humanely" toward them. Was that even possible in the midst of an inhuman system?

At one point, after he had again been listening to Elser play the zither, Fachner was overcome by curiosity. "Did you actually do it on your own, the attack in Munich?" he suddenly blurted out. "I mean, without helpers?"

Elser sat down on his plank-bed. "I can tell you, since it's in every transcript anyhow: I did it on my own. I had to do it, because Hitler was and is the downfall of Germany."

He stood up and walked to the cell window. Then he turned around to face Fachner. "You know, I'm no die-hard communist. I knew I was taking a big risk—and now I'm sitting here and waiting for them to execute me."

Fachner saw that Elser's hands were trembling and gave him a cigarette. Elser reached for it eagerly. He then went back to the table, sat down, and lit the cigarette.

"Now I have a question for you," he said, to Fachner's surprise. "You must know all about it. What is actually easiest to endure: a gassing, a hanging, or a shot in the back of the neck? I mean, which causes the least suffering?"

Fachner was horrified and searched for words. "But, Herr Elser, you have been interned for such a long time. You are handled with kid gloves. Nothing will happen to you."

Elser interrupted him. "Don't tell me that. I know better. I'm not going to be alive much longer."

Fachner silently left the cell. The situation struck him as strange. Thousands were dying in this camp from medical experiments; only a few hundred yards from the *Kommandan-turarrest*, people were beaten to death and tortured. And yet these terrible facts bounced off him. He suppressed the brutal everyday reality; he pushed it away. But here, in the prison, he had a direct relationship with the inmates. He spoke to them; he was confronted with their fears, hopes, and desires. He did not see them as anonymous prisoners, but as individual inmates. He had a secret respect for many of them; for some, he even felt sympathy. Georg Elser was one of them. The question he had asked unsettled him.

Fachner went back to his office. He thought about Elser's words. "I believed I was doing something good. Now I have to bear the consequences," he had told him as he left the cell.

Like most of the "special prisoners" in the block, Elser was afraid—afraid of the end, afraid for his life. Though the camp leaders did everything they could to leave the prisoners in the dark about the true situation of the war, many in the camp also knew by now how things were going for Germany. Some SS guards had dropped hints; prisoners in the so-called "priest block," in which oppositional priests from all over the world were interned, had received information via secret channels of the camp resistance that the war would soon be over and the Americans were only sixty miles from Dachau.

The prisoners were faced with the fear that the SS would now order more mass killings in order to erase all traces of the annihilation. Germany's cities had been reduced to rubble; the "Thousand-Year Reich" sank deeper into ruin with each passing day. Hitler and the National Socialists had brought misery, suffering, and death upon millions of people—not only in the Reich, but also in the rest of Europe. The national frenzy of joy had long since turned into a horrible dance of death.

And yet there were still fanatical supporters of National Socialism, who even now, under the hail of bombs from the enemy's planes, denounced any "comrade" and invoked the threat of death for anyone who dared to publicly oppose this madness. They occupied positions in town halls, administrative offices, police stations, and courts. They were as active in the Swabian Alps as they were in Stuttgart or Berlin. A people of triumphant enthusiasts had turned into a disillusioned, insecure people devoid of identity. But in the eyes of the National Socialists, it was still necessary to salvage what they could. Here in Dachau, in concrete terms, that meant erasing the traces.

Shortly before the end of the war, on April 5, 1945, an express letter from the chief of the security police in Berlin—recorded under file number 42/45—reached the commandants of the Dachau concentration camp. It read:

> . . . *The matter of our special protective custody prisoner Elser has also been discussed again at the highest level. The following directive has been issued: During one of the next terror attacks on Munich or in the vicinity of Dachau, Elser will purportedly meet an accidental death. To this end, when such an occasion arises, I ask you to liquidate Elser in an absolutely inconspicuous manner. I ask you to ensure that only very few people, who are bound to secrecy, are informed of this. The message to me that this has been accomplished would then read something like: "On . . . during the terror attack on . . . the protective custody prisoner Elser was fatally injured."*

In Dachau, these instructions were carried out to the letter.

"You have to go to an interrogation," Fachner told Elser on the evening of April 9, as he fetched him from the cell.

"Do I have to bring anything with me?" Elser asked, surprised at this command.

"No, you'll be right back," Fachner said, playing dumb. He knew he was lying. A few minutes ago, an SS man had given him the order to bring Elser to an "interrogation." As he said this, he had winked and smiled at him. Fachner suspected that this was the end of Georg Elser.

After the war—as a concentration camp guard, Fachner would be among those called to account and would serve a prison sentence—he recalled Elser's last walk.

> *He was led away by us along the electrically charged fence. He passed the camp gate and then crossed the camp. Then came a stone wall with a small iron door. Behind it was the crematorium. It was an inconspicuous building. In the front building of the crematorium sat an SS-Unterscharführer, who said to those entering, "Come with me." Then he led them into the execution*

room. Everyone executed by us had to undress. The person in question was told that this was in order to bathe. When the prisoner was naked and at some point happened to turn his back, he was shot unexpectedly. Elser must have been killed in the same way.

I myself was not present, but people talked about it in the camp. Oberscharführer Fritz, whom I asked about Elser's last minutes, said that Elser had been hanged from a meat hook and then incinerated in the crematorium. Incidentally, shortly after Elser was executed, Oberscharführer Fritz came to the Kommandanturarrest. *He took the zither that Elser had made for himself. I saw him walk down the corridor. On the way out, he brushed his thumb over the strings.*

On April 29, 1945, at around 5:15 PM, the first American soldiers—among them a reporter from *The New York Times*—drove a Jeep onto the grounds of the Dachau concentration camp. The escaped prisoner Karl Riemer, at the behest of the underground camp committee, had managed to make his way to the American troops at Pfaffenhofen an der Ilm and had persuaded the American commanders to advance toward Dachau instead of Munich. 32,332 prisoners, including inmates from other camps, were waiting to be delivered from their suffering.

From 1933 to 1945, at least 31,000 people had been killed in the Dachau concentration camp. Thousands had been fighting typhus and starvation since November 1944. On April 26 and 27, about 7,000 prisoners had been driven on a notorious death march toward the Ötztal Alps, where they were to build a mountain fortress. The SS had abandoned the plan of destroying the camp with all the inmates and had instead organized the evacuation in accordance with Himmler's instructions. Himmler had ordered that no prisoner was permitted to fall into the hands of the Allies. Grouped into five "marching columns," the 7,000 prisoners had set off, knowing that they could expect no mercy from the SS. Whoever fell and could not get up was shot. Numerous prisoners managed to escape. Most of the SS men had fled; some of them, wearing prisoners' uniforms, were captured.

For thousands, April 29 was the day of liberation and salvation. But for Georg Elser, the liberators arrived twenty days too late.

Georg Elser, a Man without Ideology

When this book first came out in Germany in 1993, most Germans did not care to know much about their resistance fighters. Those who were committed to opposing Hitler reminded them of their own complicity—of cowardice, opportunism, and indifference. A man like Georg Elser confronted them with their guilty conscience—provided they had one.

At the time of the writing of this book, about 6.4 million adult German citizens—nearly as many people as then lived in Baden-Württemberg, Elser's native state—still had a favorable opinion of Adolf Hitler. Another 5.5 million thought "neither positively nor negatively" about the man who had survived Elser's assassination attempt in the Munich Bürgerbräu Beer Hall on November 8, 1939. Within twelve years, he had first expanded the German Reich to the Meuse and beyond the Memel and then destroyed it. More than anyone before him, he had brought jubilation and then suffering to the Germans. And yet a survey by the magazine *Der Spiegel* from March 1989 showed clearly that, forty-four years after the end of the Third Reich, many Germans still refused to correct their image of Hitler and National Socialism.

When Philipp Jenninger spoke ambiguously about the Nazi past in 1988 as president of Germany's parliament, he had been forced to resign. But what was to be done with a hard kernel of unambiguous thinking in the people?

167

"We are not a lost cause," Franz Schönhuber, the leader of an extreme right-wing party, paradoxically called *Die Republikaner*, claimed in 1987, "but the enduring cause of the future." This came from a man who was fond of publicly vaunting his membership in the Waffen-SS.

In Germany, votes could be won with the rehabilitation of the Waffen-SS, but honoring resistance fighters didn't get you any votes.

In the political atmosphere of that time, the sad fate of Georg Elser was not only that of a failed assassin, but also that of a resister who was almost shockingly unknown—among the left as much as the right. Elser shared this fate with most who had opposed the Nazis, whose story had never particularly interested the postwar German people.

Another reason for Elser's obscurity might be that the historians' guild had long evaluated him no differently than the Gestapo had, assuming that an individual assassin must have been either hired or mad.

In actuality, Elser was anything but a fanatic or a lunatic. Rather, he was a reserved individualist who led an ordinary life. Politics, as soon as it left the everyday realm or took off on ideological flights, did not interest him. He never understood politics in the abstract sense. He believed, however, that conditions in Germany "could be changed only through an elimination of the current leadership," by which he meant Hitler, Göring, and Goebbels. He hoped that after the elimination of those "at the very top," more moderate men would step in—men who would not conquer other countries, but would improve the lot of the working class. That was the meaning of his deed.

A fastidious craftsman who called himself an "artistic carpenter" and provided only high-quality workmanship, Elser had to watch from the middle of the 1930s onward as standards were lowered due to mass production. It was not only his political worldview, but also his concept of work that was shattered by National Socialism.

Elser came from the eastern Swabian Alps, a region of Württemberg that is a bastion of Pietism. He was devout in that he had a strong sense of justice. When he attended church—whether Catholic or protestant—it was to gain peace and strength in prayer. For him, churches were places of meditation. In the days of his attack preparations, he often went to churches in Munich—alone, in communion with God.

Elser was the type who preferred to be his own master. Conformity and enthusiasm for the national hysteria were not in his nature. All this—his political opposition, his sense of justice, his deep-seated Pietistic character—gave him the energy to plan the attack for over a year, starting in the autumn of 1938, with his characteristic care and meticulousness. This was the result of a particularly difficult decision. For the Pietist, violent resistance is profoundly suspect, and assassination is a method forbidden by his religiosity. Nonetheless, Elser decided in favor of the attack and against dogmatic obstacles of his faith. He was a man with his own mind, sense of justice, and courage, surrounded by an ocean of cowardice.

* * *

Georg Elser cannot be described as a hero. His biography is the story of a simple courageous man who opposed the Nazi terror system—a man who took action. A deed like that provokes legends. The Munich prosecutor's office, however, which from 1946 to 1950 investigated the circumstances surrounding Elser's murder in Dachau, came to the conclusion that he had not been following anyone else's orders. That was based not only on intensive questioning of his family members, but also on the analysis of the transcripts of his interrogations in the Reichssicherheitshauptamt, which were found in the ruins of the Reich Ministry of Justice. Today, those transcripts are held in the federal archives in Koblenz. In the late 1960s, the records were once again studied minutely and diligently by the two Munich historians Anton Hoch and Lothar Gruchmann, so that Elser now seemed vindicated at last against all attempts to turn him into a pathological glory seeker or an agent "hired" by the National Socialists. The two historians published the results of their research in 1970 under the title *Autobiographie eines Attentäters* (*Autobiography of an Assassin*). A year earlier, the television movie *Der Attentäter* (*The Assassin*) had been filmed, and it was broadcast several times in the period that followed. Thus anyone interested in the subject had access to the persuasive evidence that Elser acted of his own volition, at his own risk, and without any conspirators or helpers. What explained, then, the persistence of the suspicion that Elser had carried out the attack at the behest of the Gestapo?

The National Socialists never put Elser on trial. Instead, he was transferred to the Sachsenhausen and Dachau concentration camps as a "special prisoner." Because the Nazi regime planned to use him in a show trial after the end of the war, Elser enjoyed special privileges for years during his internment in the camps. The Nazis envisioned a propagandistic tribunal in "liberated" London, where they would decry the participation of the British secret service. Not until April 9, 1945—when Germany's imminent defeat made the prospect of a show trial illusory—was Elser murdered in Dachau in accordance with instructions from "the highest level." What conclusion the interrogations in Munich and Berlin had ultimately reached thus remained unknown beyond the end of the war.

Not even Elser's fellow prisoners could make sense of the small, taciturn man from the eastern Swabian Alps. What those of them who survived the camp said about him after their liberation in 1945 was clearly a mixture of rumor and conjecture based on hints and evasive answers, as is common in every prison. Even Martin Niemöller later admitted that he had followed a rumor and speculation when he had publicly expressed the suspicion that Elser had been put up to the deed by the Gestapo. The investigations by the prosecutor's office in 1950 and the extensive research of the two Munich historians Hoch and Gruchmann in 1970 should have put to rest theories about the "hired" agent of the Gestapo. Nonetheless, speculations, doubts, and legends persisted.

* * *

Elser thus shared the same fate as other assassins from among the people. In the one-sided prominence given to the men of the July 20 plot in the history of opposition to Hitler, the resistance of the little people—the nameless—was largely forgotten. How could a man without an education, a simple journeyman carpenter, measure up to the great men of the July 20 conspiracy, such as Claus von Stauffenberg?

Until recently, Elser was a mere shadow in the ranks of the German resistance. Unlike Stauffenberg, who was four years older than he was, Elser was ill-suited for the role of the glorified hero. Stauffenberg was an educated officer, who initially served the National Socialist regime and only later turned against it, but then took decisive action. Elser, on the other hand, was an aloof, reserved journeyman carpenter with only a primary school diploma. And yet in 1939, when Stauffenberg and millions of other Germans still supported the Führer, Elser had already recognized the murderous character of the regime and decided to undertake the assassination.

Stauffenberg regarded himself first and foremost as a soldier, in keeping with centuries of family tradition. Though he would later lose all enthusiasm for National Socialism, he had nothing but contempt for parliamentary democracy throughout his lifetime. His sense of morality was a conglomeration of Catholic doctrine, an aristocratic code of honor, the ethos of ancient Greece, and German Romantic poetry. His bold decision to kill Hitler with a bomb was an expression of military considerations more than moral ones. The fact that Hitler by chance escaped with his life, the hopeless situation of the conspirators, the hasty execution of Stauffenberg—all this is a profound tragedy. Claus von Stauffenberg was a brave patriot—but also a strict anti-democrat.

Of interest in this connection are the comments of Ian Kershaw, who is among the most respected historians of National Socialism in Germany, which has been the focus of his work for almost forty years. In an interview about his book *The End: The Defiance and Destruction of Hitler's Germany, 1944–45,* he remarks that the unsuccessful attack on Hitler on July 20, 1944, led to a strengthening of the Nazi regime, at least temporarily: "There was a noticeable increase in Hitler's popularity with the public. The shock effect of the attack was enormous, as we can see from many private records. But even more important is the fact that a purge of the officer corps in the Wehrmacht ensued. Arch-loyalists replaced people who were considered unreliable. All resistance was ruled out as a result" (*Der Spiegel*, No. 46, 2011).

The fact that failed assassination attempts on Hitler were massively exploited by Nazi propagandists in order to invoke the invincibility of the Führer and nurture the myth of providence protecting him is historically documented. The efforts of the Gestapo and special courts to ensure that all participants and suspects were hunted down, arrested, and murdered were not directed at the officers of the July 20 plot alone.

After Georg Elser's failed attack, his hometown community in Königsbronn came under scrutiny by Nazi investigators searching for possible supporters and confidants. Until after the war—indeed, into the mid-1970s—Elser was for that reason not always an admired figure in his native region. There were many who had little sympathy for his act solely because, back then, "people got dragged into the affair who had nothing to do with it." There were admirers and critics. And fifty years after the end of the Second World War, they remained irreconcilably opposed.

There's no question about it: Elser was a challenge not only for his native region, but also for the German public as a whole. He made clear that a simple man from among the people could muster the courage for a world-historical act. He gave the lie to all those who still tried to persuade themselves that there was nothing they could have done to oppose the Nazi state. His deed made many Germans feel ashamed.

Elser had always been a loner. He sympathized with the labor movement and the Communist Party without being a member. He could not be made out to be a committed or exemplary comrade. He had little interest in ideological matters. How was such a man to be publicly recognized? How was he to be remembered? Remembrance often requires a group to sustain it; the memories of the aristocratic, military, social democratic, communist, and church resistance are preserved by the aristocracy, military, party, and church. But how could Elser be classified?

In recent years, his name has finally been restored to its rightful place in the history of the German resistance, appearing in school textbooks from which it was notably absent when this book first appeared. More than forty streets and squares and three schools have been named after him, and in 2003, the German post office even issued a special Georg Elser stamp.

In Munich there was controversy about how to memorialize Elser's act for forty years before the city finally managed to honor him. Now each evening at 9:20 PM—the time of the explosion—a red neon sign lights up on a school. Since 2010, his hometown has commemorated him with a steel memorial. It is over six feet tall and stands at the train station of the Swabian town. In the Berlin government quarter, on the bank of the Spree River, there is a bust of Elser on the Strasse der Erinnerung ("Street of Memory"), alongside Thomas Mann, Edith Stein, and Walter Rathenau, the assassinated foreign minister of the Weimar Republic. And now, as of November 2011, there is a sculpture in the middle of the old government district on Wilhelmstrasse, a steel band over fifty feet high with a string of lights sketching Elser's profile. The initiators around the writer Rolf Hochhuth intend the silhouette near Adolf Hitler's former bunker to "rise above the site of the perpetrators." The chance passerby who does not recognize Elser and might not even have heard of him learns from a small information board who is being honored here. The "symbol of reflection" (*Denkzeichen*, Hochhuth's term for the memorial) with the curved neon lights has turned out somewhat advertisement-like; the individual becomes visible only at a second glance. Georg Elser, the reclusive man who decided to resist, has once again remained anonymous.

Meanwhile, critics of the growing memorialization of Elser assert that he has become a figure of identification because he lends himself more to "self-reassurance" than, say, the aristocratic officer Stauffenberg, a highly conservative politician such as Carl Friedrich Goerdeler, or even members of communist resistance cells like the

Rote Kapelle. Elser, such critics argue, now serves as an optimal projection screen for all retroactive opposition against National Socialism;
he is ideally suited as a model for all the "contemporary do-gooders"
who act as if one's declaration of admiration for Elser and his deed
were in itself a courageous attitude.

That changes nothing about Elser's honorable character. At the latest since the former German Chancellor Helmut Kohl—a man who
once participated in a wreath-laying ceremony at an SS military ceme-
tery with his official guest Ronald Reagan—paid public tribute to Elser,
the question "To whom does Elser belong?" has been obsolete.

The historian Joseph Peter Stern once called Elser a "man without
ideology." To that, there is nothing to add.

Chronology

1903: Johann Georg Elser is born on January 4 in Hermatingen, in the Heidenheim district, the first of four children of the lumber merchants Ludwig and Maria Elser.

1904: The family moves to Königsbronn.

1910-1917: Elser attends primary school in Königsbronn.

1917-1919: Begins an apprenticeship as a lathe operator in the Königsbronn ironworks; breaks off the apprenticeship for health reasons.

1919-1922: Carpentry apprenticeship in Königsbronn.

1922: Passes journeyman's exam at the vocational school in Heidenheim at the top of his class. Works as a journeyman carpenter in the workshop of his master.

1923: Journeyman carpenter at a furniture company in Aalen.

Autumn 1923: Elser quits his job due to inflation and helps his parents with logging and farming work in exchange for free room and board.

Summer 1924-Spring 1925: Job in a furniture workshop in Heidenheim.

February 1925: Elser leaves home and works as a cabinetmaker in Bernried.

August 1925-Spring 1930: Carpenter at the Konstanz clock factory Upper Rhenish Clock Manufacturing.

1928/1929: Joins the Red Front Fighters League.

1930: Joins the Upper Rhenish Traditional Costume Society.

1930-1932: Carpenter at a clock factory in Meersburg on Lake Constance. Laid off in the spring of 1932, due to bankruptcy of the company.

Spring 1932: Returns to Königsbronn to help his mother on the farm.

1933: Joins the Königsbronn music club.

1936: Job in a Königsbronn carpenter's workshop where, among other things, desks for the Wehrmacht are produced. Elser quits due to insufficient hourly wage.

December 1936-March 1939: Works in a fittings factory in Heidenheim, first as an unskilled laborer in the fettling shop and then as an inspector of incoming material in the shipping department. He learns of the "special department" of the company, which produces armaments.

Autumn 1938: During the Sudeten crisis, Elser decides to carry out an attack against the leadership of the Nazi Party.

November 8, 1938: Travels to Munich and participates as an onlooker in the events in the city center and in the Bürgerbräu Beer Hall, in order to research the local conditions for his plan.

April 1939: Unskilled laborer in Königsbronn quarry; he obtains blasting caps.

May 1939: Accident at work: fracture of the left foot. On sick leave, considers the technical problem of transferring a clock mechanism to a detonation device. Experiments with explosives in his parents' orchard.

July 1939: Finishes design of the explosive device.

August 1939: Moves to Munich—first to Blumenstrasse 19, later to Türkenstrasse 94.

September–November 1939: Elser works thirty to thirty-five nights on the gallery of the Bürgerbräu to prepare the column above the lectern for the installation of the bomb. During the day, he works on the design of the device. He has the necessary component parts produced in various workshops.

November 1, 1939: Plants the device in the hollowed-out cavity in the column.

November 2, 1939: Plants the remaining gunpowder, explosive cartridges, blasting caps, and rifle ammunition in the hollow in the column.

November 5, 1939: Participates in a dance in the Bürgerbräu. Afterward, he finishes the installation and setting of the clocks for detonation on November 8, 1939, at 9:20 PM.

November 6, 1939: Visits his sister in Stuttgart in order to leave his belongings with her.

November 7, 1939: Travels to Munich; inspects the explosive chambers and the clock mechanism.

November 8, 1939: Travels to Konstarz.

8:45 PM: Arrest in the garden of the Wessenbergian children's home.

9:20 PM: Explosion of the bomb.

10:00 PM: Elser is brought to the Konstanz Border Commissariat and transferred to Munich.

November 13-14, 1939: Elser makes a full confession in the presence of Nebe (Reichskriminaldirektor) and Huber (SS-Obersturmbannführer, Regierungsrat, and Kriminalrat).

November 14, 1939: Transfer to the Reichssicherheitshauptamt/ Gestapo headquarters in Berlin.

November 19-23, 1939: Interrogation.

1939-1944: Special prisoner in Sachsenhausen concentration camp.

Late 1944/April 1945: Dachau concentration camp—section for privileged prisoners (*Kommandanturarrest*).

April 5, 1945: Himmler's directive to kill the "protective custody" prisoner Georg Elser.

April 9, 1945: Murder of Georg Elser.

Sources

In this book, I have attempted to describe Georg Elser's life story as authentically as possible in a documentary/narrative form. Wherever dialogue or the description of thoughts and feelings has been employed, these are products of the author's imagination. The italicized passages are all documentary; some of them have been abridged for the purposes of this story.

For reasons of privacy, all names—excluding those of historical figures and Elser's family members—have been changed.

To reconstruct Georg Elser's life and times, I availed myself of an abundance of archival material, essays, and books. I would like to cite here the books and documents that were particularly helpful to me during my work.

Albrecht, Ulrike: *Das Attentat. Über Georg Elser und das Attentat auf Hitler im Bürgerbräukeller am 8. November 1939. Mit einem Vorwort zum Hitlerputsch im November 1923 von Hermann Wilhelm*, Munich 1987.

Antoni, Ernst: *KZ—von Dachau bis Auschwitz*, Frankfurt 1979.

Davidson, Eugene: *Wie war Hitler möglich?* Rastatt 1987.

Domarus, Max: *Hitler, Reden und Proklamationen: 1932-1943*, Munich 1965.

Fest, Joachim C.: *Hitler: Eine Biographie*, Berlin 1973.

Graml, Hermann (Ed.): *Widerstand im Dritten Reich: Probleme, Ereignisse, Gestalten*, Frankfurt am Main 1984.

Gruchmann, Lother: *Georg Elser: Autobiografie eines Attentäters*, Stuttgart 1989.

Janssen, Karl-Heinz: *30. Januar: Der Tag, der die Welt veränderte*, Rastatt 1988.

Majer, Gerhard: *Schorsch: Der Attentäter aus dem Volk*, Heidenheim 1989
Peters, Lothar: *Der Hitler-Attentäter Georg Elser. Eine biographische Studie*, Cologne 1987 (unpublished manuscript).
Roon, Ger van: *Widerstand im Dritten Reich*, Munich 1987.
Rürup, Reinhard (Ed.): *Topographie des Terrors: Gestapo, SS und Reichs-sicherheitshauptamt auf dem "Prinz-Albrecht-Gelände"—Eine Dokumen-tation*, Berlin 1987.
Tuchel, Johann/Schattenfroh, Reinhold: *Zentrale des Terrors. Prinz-Albrecht-Str. 8: Hauptquartier der Gestapo*, Berlin 1987.
Zahl, Peter Paul: *Johann Georg Elser: Ein deutsches Drama*, Berlin 1982.

Also helpful for my work was the television movie *Der Attentäter* by Rainer Erler, Bavaria Film GmbH, Munich 1969.

I have occasionally quoted from the following sources or was guided by descriptions and accounts in them. I am providing these as annotations to the chapters. All quotes in the book from German-language sources are translated by Ross Benjamin:

Chapter One: The basis of the descriptions is the testimony of the customs officer Xaver R. from October 23, 1950; see Insitut für Zeitgeschichte (IfZ), Munich, call number ZS/A 17-30.
Chapter Two: For the reports of the eyewitnesses as well as Hitler's speech on November 8, 1936, see Domarus, *Hitler.* The descriptions of the Munich events on November 8, 1923, are drawn from the essay "Der Hitlerputsch" by Hermann Wilhelm in *Das Attentat* by Ulrike Albrecht. Davidson's *Wie war Hitler möglich?* was also used as a source.
Chapter Three: Substantial portions are based on testimony of the former police detective Otto G. (IfZ, call number ZS/A 17-11). The testimony of the waitress Maria S. can also be found in the IfZ, Munich.
Chapter Four: The passages from the November 9, 1939 edition of the *Münchner Neueste Nachrichten* are quoted from *Zeitmagazin*, no. 46, 1979. Reports of the "German News Agency" are excerpted from IfZ, call number ZS/A 17-6. For the reports on the internal political situation, see IfZ, Munich, call number ZS/A 17-5. The internal political stocktaking is a summary from Ulrike Albrecht, *Das Attentat*, as is the cross section of reports from the foreign press.

Chapter Five: The description of the interrogation is based on the report "Der Attentäter," *Stern,* May 3, 1964, as is the testimony of the landlady. References to speculations about contact between Otto Strasser and Georg Elser are based on the work of Lothar Peters, *Der Hitler-Attentäter Georg Elser.*

Chapter Six: Torture methods of the Gestapo are described by Johannes Tuchel and Reinhold Schattenfroh in their book *Zentrale des Terrors.* The interrogation transcript of Elser's mother from June 19, 1950, can be found under the call number ZS-A 17-9 in the IfZ, Munich, as can the excerpted testimony of his brother Leonhard (IfZ, ZS/A 17-8).

Chapter Seven: All excerpted testimony of Georg Elser can be found in the copies of the interrogation transcript, preserved as a "state secret" in the files of the Nazi ministry of justice and later in the federal archives in Koblenz under the call number R22/3100. The transcripts used in this book of Elser's testimony to the Gestapo from November 19 to 23, 1939, were first published in their entirety in the book *Autobiographie eines Attentäters,* edited by Lothar Gruchmann (Stuttgart 1970), which was reissued in 1989. All quotes from the interrogation transcripts of Elser's family members are excerpted from the extensive archival material at the Institut für Zeitgeschichte (call number ZS/A-17).

The historian Dr. Anton Hoch, research fellow and head of the IfZ archive until 1978, conducted years of extensive research on Elser and collected all available documents and witness transcripts. It is thanks to Anton Hoch that Elser has not been forgotten.

Chapter Eight: The report of the Landsberg prison warden from September 15, 1924, is excerpted from Joachim C. Fest's comprehensive book on Hitler. The description of the prison conditions is based on the essay "Bewährungsfrist für den Terroristen Adolf H." by Otto Gritschneder in the April 15, 1989, edition of the *Süddeutsche Zeitung,* as well as the article *"Von guter Selbstzucht und Beherrschung"* in *Der Spiegel,* no. 16, 1989, which describes Hitler's situation in the Landsberg prison.

Chapter Nine: The descriptions of the assumption of power on January 30, 1933, are based on the report *30. Januar: Der Tag, der die Welt veränderte* by Karl-Heinz Janssen. The testimony of the master carpenter Friedrich G., for whom Elser worked from July 2, 1934, to November 17, 1934, and then again from June 2, 1935, to September 21, 1935, is also excerpted from the IfZ archive (call number ZS/A 17-12). The oath of office is quoted from *Hitler* by Joachim C. Fest.

Chapter Ten: The "conspiracy theory" of the quarry owner V. was also spread in the series of articles titled *Der Attentäter* (*Stern*, May 3 and 17, 1964). The writers portrayed Karl Kuch, who was from Königsbronn and had immigrated to Swizerland in the '20s, as the initiator of the attack. Kuch, who after 1933 was allegedly involved in currency smuggling and died in a mysterious car accident with his wife on Pentecost in 1939, was supposedly opposed to Hitler and friendly with Elser. This rather liberal speculation was later emphatically refuted by the historian Anton Hoch.

Chapter Eleven: Hitler's Reichstag speech on the invasion of Poland on September 1, 1939, is quoted from the collection *Chronik 1939*, Dortmund 1988.

Chapter Twelve: The scenes in Berlin are based on transcripts of the testimony of the customs officer Xaver R. (IfZ, call number ZS/A 17-30).

Chapter Thirteen: Numbers and background information regarding the conditions and events in the Dachau concentration camp are drawn from the book *KZ—Von Dachau bis Auschwitz* by Ernst Antoni. The career of the SS guard L. is based on research material from the magazine *Stern*, which was compiled for the so-called *Stern*-Serie and archived in the IfZ in connection with the Elser documents.

Epilogue: The survey about Hitler, the Nazi era and its consequences appeared in *Der Spiegel*, no. 15, 1989. For the discussion of Elser as a resistance fighter, see the article by Claus Leggewie, "Der Mann, der es tat," in the February 20, 1982, edition of the *Frankfurter Rundschau*, which is quoted in part. The quote from Ian Kershaw is from an interview in *Der Spiegel*, No. 46, 2011. For a detailed historical comparison between Georg Elser and Claus von Stauffenberg, see my essay "Der Mann, der Hitler töten wollte" in *Cicero, Magazin für politische Kultur*, Berlin, November 2009. On the debate and the design competition in connection with a memorial for Elser in Berlin, see the October 12, 2011, press release of the Berlin Senatskanzlei as well as numerous newspaper reports, among them "Georg Elser-Denkmal in Berlin," www .spiegel-online/kultur.de, and "Denkmal für einen tragischen Helden," www.süddeutsche.de. All schools, squares, and streets in Germany named after Elser are documented at www.georg-elser .net. Further up-to-date information can be found at www.georg -elser-arbeitskreis.de. For criticism of the memorialization of Elser, see Peter Koblank's articles in "Mythos Elser" at www.georg -elser-arbeitskreis.de.

For interviews, advice and access to sources, I thank:

The Studienkreis zur Erforschung und Vermittlung der Geschichte des deutschen Widerstands 1933-1945 in Frankfurt am Main
The Institut für Zeitgeschichte, Munich
Gerhard Majer and Gertrud Schädler of the Georg Elser-Arbeitskreis in Heidenheim
The ZEIT-Archiv in Hamburg
Herr Leonhard Elser in Königsbronn
Herr Eugen Rau in Königsbronn
Frau Gabriele Göttmann in Darmstadt for her careful transcription work.

For the present English-language edition, I offer my special thanks to Ross Benjamin. I consider myself lucky to have such a detail-oriented translator. At our meetings in Berlin and New York, I particularly came to appreciate his friendly tenacity. Thanks to his work, numerous documents and passages are more comprehensible and readable. What more could an author ask for? I thank my agent Jennifer Lyons for her dedication and her excellent work in bringing the book to Skyhorse Publishing. I am grateful to the team at Skyhorse for their professionalism. They have done everything in their power to ensure that this book will find interested readers in America.

Helmut Ortner